Computational Risk Management

Editors-in-Chief

Desheng Wu, University of Chinese Academy of Sciences and Stockholm University, Beijing, Beijing, China

David L. Olson, Department of Supply Chain Management and Analytics, University of Nebraska-Lincoln, Lincoln, NE, USA

John Birge, University of Chicago Booth School of Business, Chicago, IL, USA

Risks exist in every aspect of our lives and risk management has always been a vital topic. Most computational techniques and tools have been used for optimizing risk management and the risk management tools benefit from computational approaches. Computational intelligence models such as neural networks and support vector machines have been widely used for early warning of company bankruptcy and credit risk rating. Operational research approaches such as VaR (value at risk) optimization have been standardized in managing markets and credit risk, agent-based theories are employed in supply chain risk management and various simulation techniques are employed by researchers working on problems of environmental risk management and disaster risk management. Investigation of computational tools in risk management is beneficial to both practitioners and researchers. The Computational Risk Management series is a high-quality research book series with an emphasis on computational aspects of risk management and analysis. In this series, research monographs as well as conference proceedings are published.

More information about this series at http://www.springer.com/series/8827

Desheng Dash Wu • David L. Olson

Pandemic Risk Management in Operations and Finance

Modeling the Impact of COVID-19

 Springer

Desheng Dash Wu
University of Chinese
Academy of Science
Beijing, China
Stockholm University
Stockholm, Sweden

David L. Olson
Department of Supply Chain
Management and Analytics
University of Nebraska–Lincoln
Lincoln, NE, USA

ISSN 2191-1436   ISSN 2191-1444   (electronic)
Computational Risk Management
ISBN 978-3-030-52196-7   ISBN 978-3-030-52197-4   (eBook)
https://doi.org/10.1007/978-3-030-52197-4

This Springer imprint is published by the registered company Springer Nature Switzerland AG.
The registered company address is: Gewerbestrasse 11, 6330 Cham, Switzerland

Preface

COVID-19 has hit the world hard, causing tremendous structural change. The impact on global supply chains has been severe. It has also affected financial operations. What is needed are analytic tools to aid in dealing with the impact of the pandemic on our economies. These analytic tools are not panaceas, and certainly would not cure the problems we face. But they provide the means to aid governments, firms, and individuals to cope with specific problems.

This book provides an overview of COVID-19 progression and evaluates the impact on financial and supply chain operations. Progress of COVID-19 around the globe is reviewed, followed by epidemic modeling. Sources of quantitative data as well as text data are presented. Models are applied to view the impact of the pandemic on supply chains, on macroeconomic performance, and on financial operations. Specific experiences of the Chinese banking system are related, with predictions of the impact on Swedish banking. Models related to pandemic planning include evaluation of financial contagion, debt risk analysis, and health system efficiency performance. Specific models of pandemic parameters are discussed.

Pandemics put a strain on economies, due to the need to provide medical resources as well as the need to control the population to halt disease spread. COVID-19 is expected to have a major impact in setting back global economic development. Obviously the longer lockdowns are imposed, the greater is the economic impact. If some areas of the global economy begin to recover, there might be less reticence to wait before opening up economies on the part of other regions or countries. The choice is complete safety and starvation, or coping with what nature throws at us and move on. It will be interesting to see the relative success of the two extremes on this dichotomy with respect to response to one of nature's challenges.

The book seeks to provide simple explanations and demonstration of some descriptive tools. Models are demonstrated using available data of the ongoing COVID-19 pandemic. The style of the book is intended to be descriptive, seeking to explain how methods work, with some citations, but without deep scholarly reference. The data sets and software are all selected for widespread availability and access by any reader with computer links.

This work was supported in part by the Strategic Priority Research Program of CAS under Grant XDA23020203, the National Natural Science Foundation of China under Grant 71825007, the Chinese Academy of Sciences Frontier Scientific Research Key Project under Grant QYZDB-SSW-SYS021, the CAS Strategic Research and Decision Support System Development under Grant GHJ-ZLZX-2019-33-3, Marianne and Marcus Wallenberg Foundation under Grant MMW 2015.0007, and the International Partnership Program of Chinese Academy of Sciences, Grant No.211211KYSB20180042.

Selected portions of this book or its individual chapters build upon work already published in the following articles and have been reused with due permissions of the copyright owners.

Pan, J., Ding, S., Wu, D., Yang, S., & Yang, J. (2019). Exploring behavioural intentions toward smart healthcare services among medical practitioners: A technology transfer perspective. *International Journal of Production Research, 57*(18), 5801–5820. https://www.tandfonline.com/doi/abs/10.1080/00207543.2018.1550272?scroll=top&needAccess=true&journalCode=tprs20

Wu, D., & Wu, D. D. (2019). Risk-based robust evaluation of hospital efficiency. *IEEE Systems Journal, 13*(2), 1906–1914. https://doi.org/10.1109/JSYST.2018.2865031

Wu, D. D., & Olson, D. L. (2014). A system dynamics modelling of contagion effects in accounts risk management. *Systems Research, 31*, 502–511. https://doi.org/10.1002/sres.2291

Ren, R., Wu, D. D., & Liu, T. (2019). Forecasting stock market movement direction using sentiment analysis and support vector machine. *IEEE Systems Journal, 13* (1), 760–770. https://doi.org/10.1109/JSYST.2018.2794462

Stockholm, Sweden   Desheng Dash Wu
Lincoln, NE, USA   David L. Olson

Acknowledgements

This work was supported in part by the Strategic Priority Research Program of CAS under Grant XDA23020203, the National Natural Science Foundation of China under Grant 71825007, the Chinese Academy of Sciences Frontier Scientific Research Key Project under Grant QYZDB-SSW-SYS021, Marianne and Marcus Wallenberg Foundation under Grant MMW 2015.0007, and the International Partnership Program of Chinese Academy of Sciences, Grant No.211211KYSB20180042.

Contents

1 Introduction 1
   1.1   The Nature of the Problem 1
   1.2   Alternate Approaches 3
   1.3   Conclusion 4
   References 5

2 Comparison with Past Pandemics 7
   2.1   Epidemic Impact 8
   2.2   SEIR Model 8
   2.3   Coronavirus Progress 11
   2.4   Measures 13
   2.5   Chinese Experience 14
   2.6   Conclusions 16
   References 17

3 System Dynamics Modeling of Contagion Effects 19
   3.1   Financial Contagion 20
   3.2   System Dynamics Tools 21
   3.3   Accounts Receivable Data and Model 21
        3.3.1   System Dynamics Model 22
        3.3.2   Firm Performance 23
   3.4   Results and Discussion 24
        3.4.1   Social Interaction 26
   3.5   Conclusions 29
   References 29

4 Text Mining Support to Pandemic Planning 31
   4.1   Text Mining of Financial Data 31
   4.2   Investor Sentiment 32
   4.3   Support Vector Machines 34
   4.4   Experiment 36

		4.4.1	Data Description	36
		4.4.2	Sentiment Calculation	36
		4.4.3	Prediction	38
		4.4.4	Investment Performance	42
	4.5	Conclusion	44
	References	45

5 Macroeconomic Impact 47
    5.1   Policy Options 48
    5.2   Global Response 50
    5.3   Summary 51
    References 51

6 Supply Chain Impact 53
    6.1   Pandemic Disruption 53
    6.2   Network Analysis 56
            6.2.1   SARS 57
            6.2.2   MERS 57
            6.2.3   Ebola 59
            6.2.4   COVID-19 61
    6.3   Conclusion 63
    References 63

7 Debt Risk Analysis Using Two-Tier Networks 65
    7.1   Two-Tier Counterparty Risk-Contagion Network Model 67
            7.1.1   Definition of Two-Tier Counterparty Risk-Contagion
                     Networks 67
            7.1.2   Division of Two-Tier Risk-Contagion Networks 67
            7.1.3   Measurement of an Organization's External Risk
                     Exposure (ERE) 68
    7.2   Risk-Contagion Channel: Node Degree 69
            7.2.1   Distribution of Risk-Contagion Channel: Degree
                     Distribution 69
            7.2.2   Risk-Contagion Path: Average Shortest Path 70
            7.2.3   Aggregation of Risk-Contagion Network: Clustering
                     Coefficient 70
    7.3   Regression Model 71
    7.4   Empirical Study on Nonfinancial Corporate Debt Risk
           Contagion 73
            7.4.1   Sample Data 73
            7.4.2   Construction of the First Layer Network 75
            7.4.3   Construction of the Second Layer Network 77
            7.4.4   Identify Key Risk-Contagion Nodes 80

          7.4.5   Ownership and External Guarantee Scale 83
          7.4.6   Determinants of External Risk Exposure 83
    7.5   Inferences 85
    7.6   Conclusions 87
    References 87

8   The Effect of COVID-19 on the Banking Sector 89
    8.1   Short-Term Impacts on Bank Performance Indicators 90
    8.2   Long-Term Impact on the Banking Industry Is Limited 92
    8.3   Pandemic Possibly Increases Systemic Risks in the Banking
          Industry 95
    8.4   Discussions and Suggestions 95
    8.5   Conclusions 98
    References 99

9   Assessment of Smart Healthcare Services 101
    9.1   Technology Acceptance Model 102
          9.1.1   Attitude 102
          9.1.2   Perceived Usefulness 102
          9.1.3   Perceived Ease of Use 102
          9.1.4   Subjective Norm 103
          9.1.5   Perceived Risk 103
    9.2   Technology Transfer 104
    9.3   Department Difference 106
    9.4   Research Methodology 108
          9.4.1   Measurements 108
          9.4.2   Data Collection 108
          9.4.3   Data Analysis and Results 109
    9.5   Measurement Model 109
          9.5.1   Reflective Measurement Evaluation 109
          9.5.2   Formative Measurement Evaluation 112
          9.5.3   Measurement Invariance Assessment 114
          9.5.4   Hypotheses Testing and Multigroup Analysis 115
    9.6   Discussion and Implications 118
          9.6.1   Theoretical Implications 119
    9.7   Conclusion 119
    References 120

10 Healthcare Efficiency Modeling 123
    10.1   Nominal and Robust DEA Models 124
          10.1.1 Basic CCR Model 124
          10.1.2 Robust DEA Model 125
    10.2   Efficiency Analysis for US Hospitals 127
          10.2.1 Data 127

10.3   Results and Analysis   132
10.4   Conclusion   134
References   135

11 Recapitulation   137
11.1   Problem Background   137
11.2   Conclusion   139
Reference   139

About the Authors

Desheng Dash Wu is a Distinguished Professor with the Economics and Management School, University of Chinese Academy of Sciences, Beijing, China, and Professor with the Stockholm Business School, Stockholm University, Sweden. He has published over 150 ISI-indexed papers in refereed journals, such as *Production and Operations Management, Decision Sciences, Risk Analysis*, and the *IEEE Transactions on Systems, Man, and Cybernetics*, and 7 books with Springer. He has been invited to give plenary lectures and keynote talks in various international conferences more than 20 times. His current research interests include mathematical modeling of systems containing uncertain and risky situations, with special interests in the finance-economics operations interface, maximizing operational and financial goals using the methodologies for game theory, and large-scale optimization. He is Elected Member of the Academia Europaea (the Academy of Europe), Elected Member of European Academy of Sciences and Arts, and Elected Member of International Eurasian Academy of Sciences. Prof. Wu was a recipient of the ten big impact articles in the *Journal of the Operational Research Society*, 2019 Elsevier Most Cited Researcher, the Top 25 Hottest Article in Elsevier Journals, and the Best Paper Award Most Cited Articles in Human and Ecological Risk Assessment. He has served as an Associate Editor and a Guest Editor for several journals, such as *Risk Analysis, IEEE Transactions on Systems, Man, and Cybernetics*, the *Annals of Operations Research, Computers and Operations Research, the International Journal of Production Economics*, and *Omega*. He serves as the book series editor on computational risk management at Springer.

David L. Olson is the James & H.K. Stuart Professor and Chancellor's Professor at the University of Nebraska. He has published research in over 200 refereed journal articles, primarily on the topic of multiple objective decision-making, information technology, supply chain risk management, and data mining. He teaches in the management information systems, management science, and operations management areas. He has authored over 40 books, to include *Decision Aids for Selection Problems, Introduction to Information Systems Project Management, Managerial*

Issues of Enterprise Resource Planning Systems, *Supply Chain Risk Management*, and *Supply Chain Information Technology*. Additionally, he has coauthored the books *Introduction to Business Data Mining*, *Enterprise Risk Management*, *Advanced Data Mining Techniques*, *Enterprise Information Systems*, *Enterprise Risk Management Models*, and *Financial Enterprise Risk Management*. He has served as associate editor of *Service Business*, *Decision Support Systems*, and *Decision Sciences* and coeditor in chief *of International Journal of Services Sciences*. He has made over 200 presentations at international and national conferences on research topics. He is a member of the Decision Sciences Institute, the Institute for Operations Research and Management Sciences, and the Multiple Criteria Decision Making Society. He was a Lowry Mays endowed Professor at Texas A&M University from 1999 to 2001. He was named the Raymond E. Miles Distinguished Scholar award for 2002 and was a James C. and Rhonda Seacrest Fellow from 2005 to 2006. He was named Best Enterprise Information Systems Educator by IFIP in 2006. He is a Fellow of the Decision Sciences Institute.

Chapter 1
Introduction

Abstract This book presents a variety of operations research modeling initiatives related to pandemic planning. This chapter briefly reviews the progress of Coronavirus disease 2019 (COVID-19) and outlines the content of the remainder of the book. COVID-19 has shut down a large part of the global economy for months since early 2020, causing health ramifications including over 100,000 deaths globally. The tools presented in this book offer a means to prepare or cope with pandemics.

Coronavirus disease 2019 (COVID-19) has had a major impact on the global economy. The virus is extremely contagious, and has resulted in the death of several thousands of people globally. The chapters we cover are motivated to present a variety of models which may aid in the analysis of some of the aspects in pandemic planning.

In this book, we review the initial stage of COVID-19 and compare it with that of the other global epidemics of the past, including the Severe Acute Respiratory Syndrome (SARS), Middle East Respiratory Syndrome (MERS), and the Ebola virus disease. We also review the control measures that were applied in the past. The impact on supply chain operations is compared to previous situations and differences as well as similarities are noted. Supply chain risks in the form of slack inventories are discussed, along with the areas of potential threats.

1.1 The Nature of the Problem

We do not want to focus on China because the virus has spread throughout the world. China experienced an outbreak of COVID-19 during late December 2019. At that time, out of the 72,314 cases reported, 44,672 were confirmed with COVID-19, based on a positive viral nucleic acid test from throat swabs; 16,186 suspected cases were not tested because of the insufficient testing capacity; 10,567 cases were clinically diagnosed without testing, based on symptoms; and 889 cases were

D. D. Wu, D. L. Olson, *Pandemic Risk Management in Operations and Finance*,
Computational Risk Management, https://doi.org/10.1007/978-3-030-52197-4_1

asymptomatic without typical symptoms of fever, dry cough, and fatigue, but tested positive on the swab test. Most cases were between 30 and 79 years old. Most cases (81%) were diagnosed with mild non-pneumonia and mild pneumonia, 14% were severe with dyspnea, high respiration rates, blood oxygen saturation, and 5% were critical with respiratory failure, septic shock, and/or multiple organ dysfunction or failure. The overall fatality rate at that time was 1023 of the 44,672 confirmed cases. None of them were 9 years of age or younger, but the fatality rate for those between 70 and 79 years of age was 8% and for those 80 years of age and older was 14.8%. China adopted strong lockdown measures to control the spread of the virus, which appear to have been effective. Health care personnel were the ones who were hard hit because of the virus.

The virus soon spread all over the world, hitting Iran and Italy heavily in March. Soon, Spain's experience surpassed that of Italy, and in April, the United States of America had the most cases in the world. Urban areas such as Milan, New York City, and Los Angeles were especially hard hit, with the local governments becoming seriously concerned about the capacity of hospital facilities. By the end of April 2020, almost the entire globe was affected, with the high potential for the spread of infection being the highly populated regions.

The World Health Organization (WHO) declared COVID-19 a world health emergency in January 2020 after it severely impacted China and South Korea. Both these countries responded with social distancing, travel restrictions, closure of shops and restaurants, cancellation of sporting events, and mandatory quarantine, effectively stopping the economic growth. On March 11, 2020, after it had made significant inroads in other countries (especially Iran, Italy and Spain), COVID-19 was officially named as a pandemic [1]. It was observed that COVID-19 was negatively impacting a broad swath of trade, especially tourism, medical supplies, consumer electronics, energy, and food. In an effort to control the spread of the virus, social distancing and the shutdown of nonessential activities was a common action, quickly placing a brake on supply chains as well as local economic activities. The closing down of global economies was expected by the Organization of Economic Cooperation and Development, which as a result lowered its forecast of global economic growth for 2020 from 2.9 to 2.4%, given that the virus peaked in the first quarter of 2020. Since the spread of the virus is continuing even after the first quarter, more dismal forecasts are being made. The unemployment rate has skyrocketed in the US, while the stock markets have been fluctuating around 83% of where they were after an initial drop of almost a third. Although central banks have taken a number of emergency measures, the market reaction to them has not been appreciative and a further drop in the trading price is being witnessed. Meanwhile, most US states declared a shutdown of nonessential businesses.

The Congressional Research Service [1] compared the current crisis with the 2008 housing mortgage crisis. The 2008 crisis was rooted in the structural weakness of the US financial sector, with a bubble blamed on the impossibility for firms to identify the demands. On the contrary, the 2020 crisis began as a supply shock. The more tightly knit global economy consists of highly connected international supply chains for the most part, to a greater degree than ever before. In January 2020, plant closings led to interruptions of supply chains and concerns about depleting inventories. Uncertainties on the ability to control the spread of the virus as well as of the effectiveness of public policies halted most of the economic activity, reducing demand to complement the reduction of supply. The economic effects of the pandemic quickly had lots of impact on the Chinese economy, and very soon thereafter on the European and American business activities. Concerns were voiced that COVID-19 could trigger a wave of defaults around the world [2].

McKinsey & Company [3] observed that the virus spread worldwide despite the containment efforts. However, the spread was very difficult to be measured accurately. In USA, the governmental reaction was "testing, testing, testing"—and, of course, since "you shall find if you seek," the US statistics of April 1, 2020 show more cases in the US than anywhere else in the world. Of course, many other countries with lesser number of testing equipments may be undercounting, while the US may be overcounting. Italy reported over 11,500 deaths due to COVID-19 by the end of March 2020, compared to about 2400 reported by the US in late April 2020. Iran, Spain, and France were also hard hit. While McKinsey & Company attributed the low testing rate to be a likely factor in the spread of virus in Italy, it has opined that the relative success experienced by South Korea (with 162 deaths as of March 31, 2020) was because of the aggressive testing, contact tracing and surveillance, and mandatory quarantine. Sweden stood out with a different strategy, with less rigid social control. There has been significant debate as to the wisdom of this approach, with the medical technocracy decrying it while supporters point to benefits of less economic and social sacrifice while relying on human system development of immunity. Thus, there are vastly different results reported across the world, but it appears to us that the virus is just beginning to hit large-population centers in Africa and Eastern Europe.

1.2 Alternate Approaches

China was hit by COVID-19, so had to face the challenge without warning. The governmental reaction was border closures, city-level lockdowns for several places, quarantines and shelter-in-place restrictions, and mandatory closure of businesses. Some US states are adopting this approach, which seems most appropriate for high-burden environments. USA has stressed on widespread testing, at least within available testing units. France has adopted national lockdown with strict police enforcement, along with targeted as opposed to widespread testing. Spain, which has been very hard hit, has adopted a national lockdown limiting nonessential movement. Spain has reported limited testing capabilities. The UK adopted a strategy focusing on scaled testing while avoiding lockdowns, although by March 20, 2020 they started enforcing lockdowns. Italy, which has suffered the most deaths to date, imposed strict regional and national lockdowns early, as well as much more testing than other European countries. At the other extreme, the South Korea model (which seems most appropriate for low-to-medium burden environments) applied aggressive testing of suspected cases along with contact tracing and isolation, and enforced quarantine. Norway adopted a similar strategy, adopting drive-through testing as soon as the first case was identified, along with enforced quarantine.

The overall strategy recommended by McKinsey & Company involved life safeguards through suppression as quickly as possible, expanded treatment and testing capacity, and research for vaccines or other cure. Economic safeguards were to support the people and businesses affected, get them ready to return to work once the virus was safely abated, and prepare to improve upon the expected 8–13% drop in the economic output.

Supply chain impact has been severe. Our more interlocked economy depends upon parts from around the globe for many products. The initial fears were from loss of sources. However, that quickly shifted to the realization that demand was dropping around the globe, and social distancing was also forcing plant shutdowns (as well as many entertainment, travel, and restaurant businesses), which has created vast revenue shortfalls. Banking systems around the world are pumping money to support businesses as well as for paying the unemployed. We see some massive changes induced by the COVID-10 experience. Production facilities will be even more encouraged to automate, which may jeopardize many manual labor jobs. In addition, incentives are in place for supply chains to encourage local sources.

The McKinsey report cited notes that as of late March, about 80% of plants have been reopened, indicating that China views that they are in the recovery phase. But, supply chains will be disrupted by quarantines and other restrictions. Meanwhile, demand has been massively impacted.

On the financial side, governments have reacted vigorously to pump money into the economy to salvage businesses and to provide ample unemployment benefits. These measures have created issues with the fiscal limits of capacity, which may be problematic later. The economic effects of COVID-19 are having a significant impact on European business activity, with the threat of deep economic recession [4].

1.3   Conclusion

COVID-19 is clearly different from SARS or MERS, although all the three belong to the same virus family. SARS and MERS were more deadly per case, but were nowhere nearly as contagious. COVID-19 has rapidly spread across the globe, bringing the entire global economy to its knees. The impact has ramifications we do not yet know. We hope that we can cope and recover, in fact most expect that we will. However, meanwhile, the economy has been put on hold, and massive numbers of people have found themselves unemployed. Governments are trying to mitigate this problem, but are never very efficient at equitably distributing the benefits.

The need of the hour is the analytic tools to aid in dealing with the impact of the pandemic on our economies. These analytic tools are not panaceas, and certainly will not cure the problems we face. But, they provide means to aid governments, firms, and individuals to cope with specific problems.

Our book seeks to look at the operations (supply chain) and financial impact of the COVID-19 pandemic. Chapter 2 reviews the past epidemics and compared them with the current crisis. We then present a series of models useful and appropriate for pandemic planning. Chapter 3 presents a system dynamics model of a financial contagion. Chapter 4 looks at data sources, to include text data available from sources such as Google and Baidu. Chapter 5 considers the impact on the macroeconomic system while Chap. 6 focuses on the supply chain impact. Chapter 7 looks at the impact of the pandemic on the supply chain financial operations. Chapter 8 analyzes the impact of COVID-19 on the banking sector using, to include impact on credit demand and potential for recession, as well as impact on particular industries. Chapter 8 looks at the operational-level impact of information technology on the medical system. Chapter 9 follows with comparative analysis through technology acceptance modeling (TAM). Chapter 10 presents the Data Envelopment Analysis (DEA) models particularly useful in the assessment of health care efficiency, to include the estimation of the rate of contagion spread, forecasting models, and the modeling of economic growth.

References

1. Congressional Research Service. (2020, March 26). *Global economic effects of COVID-19 R46270*. Congressional Research Service. https://crsreports.congress.gov
2. Plender, J. (2020, March 4). The seeds of the next debt crisis. *Financial Times*.
3. McKinsey & Company. (2020, March 25). *COVID-19: Briefing note—Global health and crisis response*. McKinsey & Company.
4. Arnold, M., & Romei, V. (2020, March 24). Business activity crashes to record low in Eurozone. *Financial Times*. https://222ft.com/content/f5ebabd4-6dad-11ea-89df-41bea055720b

Chapter 2
Comparison with Past Pandemics

Abstract This chapter reviews three recent pandemics—SARS, MERS, and Ebola, with the intent of seeing the scope of the health impact of these pandemics and the control mechanisms applied. COVID-19 is different in major ways—much more contagious, with health effects less impactful for most of the population. There is no comparison in impact, but coping with pandemics includes some commonality. Some basic pandemic statistics are reviewed.

COVID-19 shut down many Chinese operations in their efforts to control the rapid spread. This disrupted many key items for many supply chains throughout the world, as well as on travel and tourism. Airports and shipping have been shut down in some instances, stopping various participations in global supply chains. Travel also had impacted the spread of the virus worldwide. Spread was rapid, with Iran and Italy being especially hard hit in death rate, South Korea experiencing a high case rate but thankfully a lower death rate.

In the United States, there are over 10,000 reported deaths from the flu every year. COVID-19 has caused slightly over 5000 deaths in the world in the first few months. COVID-19 is highly contagious, although similar to flu in impact. But our tightly wound society expects perfection (free, perfect, and now). China was able to keep the spread of the virus under some control through drastic curtailment of human movement. In the US, professional sports and educational facilities have been shut down in a similar drastic response. This clearly places a dampener on the economy, and the stock market in its usual panic response has plunged over 30%. Meanwhile, the economy is basically otherwise sound. Whether a recession is created by the fear of COVID-19 remains to be seen.

D. D. Wu, D. L. Olson, *Pandemic Risk Management in Operations and Finance*,
Computational Risk Management, https://doi.org/10.1007/978-3-030-52197-4_2

2.1 Epidemic Impact

Epidemic sickness can rapidly spread by a group of infectious agents through several methods of interactions and threaten the health condition of a large number of people in very little time. The threat of emerging and re-emerging infectious diseases to global healthcare remains critical, and the capacity of pandemic preparedness to confront such threats is of great importance. Effective responses of an epidemic outbreak would tremendously help to stabilize economic activities and reduce systematic risks. Timely and adequate supply of critical resources in disastrous situations is a key factor in controlling communicable diseases. In order to contain epidemics before irreversible consequences occur, information channels need to be transparently managed in conjunction with financial resources from both government and social support entities. Quick response of emergency operations management in healthcare during the containment effort is of paramount importance. Ginsberg et al. [1] noted the potential of Data Analytics and Artificial Intelligence (AI)-based technologies in operation management to further the following: effective pre-emption, prevention, and combating threats of infectious disease epidemics, and facilitating understanding of health-improving behaviors and public emotions during epidemics. Today's world of seamless boundaries and global interconnectivity has generated an explosion of health data from 500 petabytes in 2012 to 25,000 petabytes in 2020 [2]. From a systems-thinking perspective, AI offers new tools for public health practitioners and policy makers to revolutionize healthcare and population health through focused, context-specific interventions and expanding access to health information and services.

Epidemics have tormented civilization since the dawn of time. A few major epidemics are listed in Table 2.1.

We discuss the immediate impact based on Chinese statistics and compare this most recent strain of coronavirus with that of some previous epidemics. We also identify some lessons learned from other epidemics over the past two decades. We consider the severe acute respiratory syndrome (SARS) of 2003, the Middle East Respiratory Syndrome (MERS) of 2012 and 2015, and the Ebola virus outbreak of 2014. We note that SARS, MERS, and Ebola had much higher death proportions than the novel coronavirus, although the World Health Organization (WHO) as well as local officials throughout the world are taking COVID-19 very seriously.

2.2 SEIR Model

SEIR (from Susceptible, Exposed, Infected, Recovered) is an extended version of SIR. Let us take a glance at the estimation of a city given by the standard SIR (from Susceptible, Infected, Recovered) model, where the infected arrives at 14 million (Fig. 2.1). The parameters are based on real data, while the curve given by SIR never fits the real data.

Table 2.1 Some salient epidemics

Epidemic	Approximate time	Comments
Black plague	1347–1351 (one of many)	75–200 million deaths in Eurasia
		1348–1350 killed 30–45% of European population
		Reduced world population from 475 million to 350–375 million
Influenza	1918–1920	500 million estimated cases
		Death toll: 20–100 million
		10–20% mortality
HIV/AIDS	1980s–current	Estimated 60 million
		36 million deaths
SARS	2002–2003	Over 8000 cases, mortality about 0.1
Swine flu	2009–2010 H1N1	60.8 million cases
		195,000 to 402,000 US hospitalizations
		8900 to 18,000 deaths
		One estimate 284,000 deaths
MERS	2012–2013	Over 1300 cases, mortality 0.34
Ebola	2013–2016	Over 28,000 cases, mortality near 0.4
COVID-19	2020	Ongoing

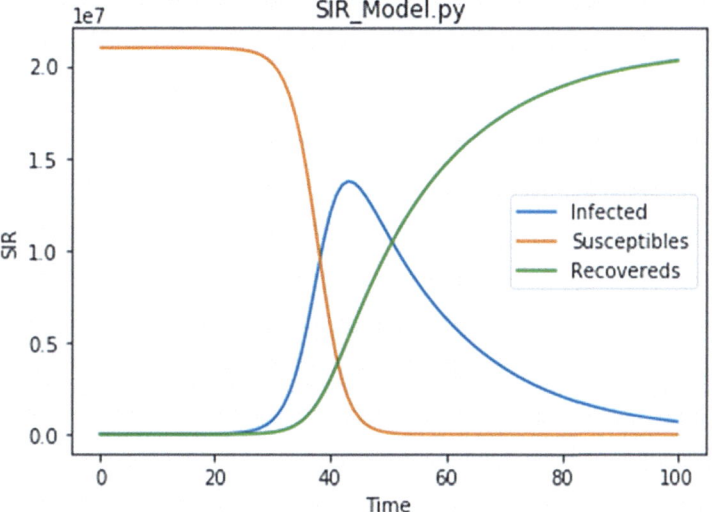

Fig. 2.1 SIR plot

Figure 2.2 gives the plot for a simulation of U.S data.

The SIR and the following SEIR model have an exponential spread period. As government intervention is not considered, by consequent of an $R_0 > 1$, all susceptible are infected and finally recovered. Apparently, death and herd immunity are not

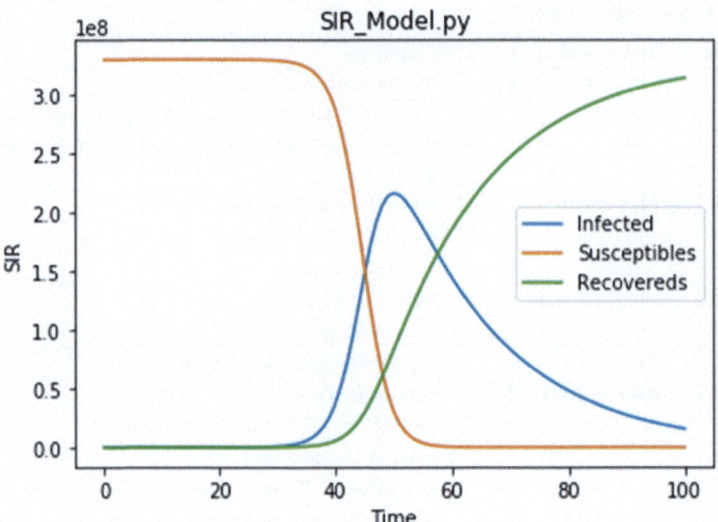

Fig. 2.2 SEIR plot for US data

involved. Indeed, the natural R_0 of COVID-19 is between 2 and 3, but with government intervention, the R_0 can be lower down to 0.04 (China).

A standard version of SEIR is given by the following equations:

$$\begin{cases} \dot{S} = \mu N - (\nu + N^{-1}\beta I)S \\ \dot{E} = N^{-1}\beta IS - (\nu + \sigma)E \\ \dot{I} = \sigma E - (\gamma + \nu)I \\ \dot{R} = \gamma I - \nu R \end{cases},$$

where S = susceptible, E = exposed, I = infectious, R = recovered, $N = S + E + I + R$ = total population number, μ = birth rate, ν = death rate, σ = incubation rate. Now, ignore the birth rate and death rate, introduce import cases instead. Also, both exposed and infectious can spread the disease (but with different rates); thus, the equations become:

$$\begin{cases} \dot{S} = \mu(1 - \rho) - N^{-1}(\beta_E E + \beta_I I)S \\ \dot{E} = \mu\rho + N^{-1}(\beta_E E + \beta_I I)S - \sigma E \\ \dot{I} = \sigma E - \gamma I \\ \dot{R} = \gamma I \end{cases},$$

where μ is the number of inflow population per time unit, ρ is the probability that the entrant is exposed.

2.3 Coronavirus Progress

The 2020 outbreak of coronavirus has been tracked. R_0 is difficult to assess during an epidemic, just as is the mortality rate because data are subject to constant change and deaths lag the onset of disease. R_0 has been estimated at about 3.5, and some estimates higher, but seem to be settling at the rate of about 1.5 based on reported Chinese data. Note that until late February they were essentially the same count. The WHO statistics on February 23, 2020 indicated 77,345 total cases in China to date, with 2593 deaths and 25,029 recovered cases. Meanwhile, while new Chinese infections seem to be tapering off, worldwide cases grow, especially in South Korea, Italy, and Iran.

Figure 2.3 gives numbers given by the WHO counting new cases by country.

China applied drastic lockdown policies, which apparently have resulted in a quick reduction in new cases. In fact, production has resumed for many manufacturing facilities. South Korea quickly contained growth in their cases. Iran suffered a growth in new cases, but about the first of April seem to have gained control in the spread. Italy was next to have the most new cases, which leveled off late March. Spain lagged Italy a bit, but have had even more new cases. Meanwhile, in late March, the US has taken over as reporting the most new cases. How much of that is due to more testing is unknown.

Figure 2.4 plots reported deaths due to COVID-19.

Figure 2.4 demonstrates the vast majority of cases until about February 20. Since then, there have been noted cases in South Korea, as well as in Italy, Iran, and Japan. Mortality has been highest in the United States. Figure 2.4 also shows the progression of the epidemic. China peaked about six weeks after initial reports and seems to have gained control another month later. Italy saw a surge in cases that is ongoing as

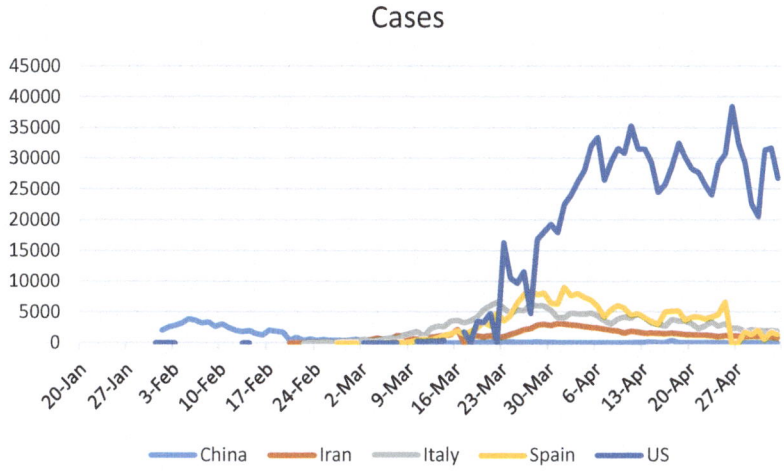

Fig. 2.3 WHO reported new cases of COVID-19

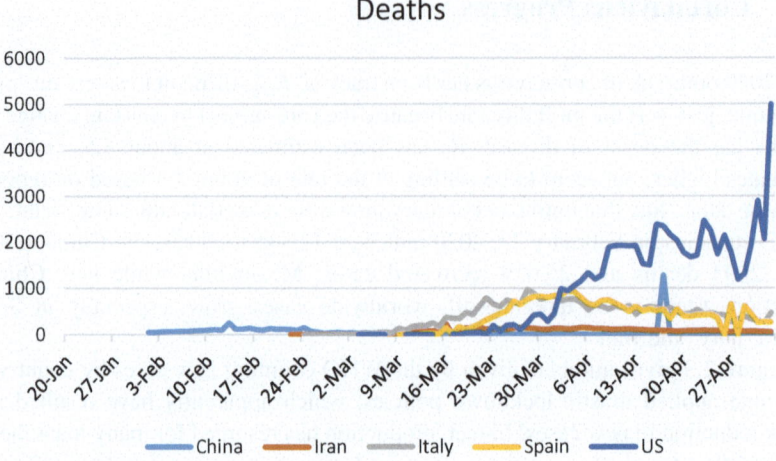

Fig. 2.4 Reports of deaths in the most impacted countries to date

of the last report, about 3 weeks after the initial report on 5 February. Iran's first report was on 20 February, and their experience in deaths surpassed that of Italy the first week in March and is approaching the total death count of China. Meanwhile, Spain is following Italy's experience. Other countries, such as South Korea and Japan, which had the earliest non-Chinese reported cases, have had low death counts. We can infer that their health systems were better able to cope with the onset of cases. Late in March, deaths appeared in large numbers in the US, which continue to grow at a fast rate. Meanwhile, vast areas of the world (Africa and South America) have not yet seen large counts but could be expected to in the second quarter of 2020.

Mortality rates are hard to measure in the early stages of an epidemic. The disease takes some time before causing death. A naïve mortality calculation would divide concurrent deaths versus cases—but that grossly understates mortality. Official mortality divides deaths by total closed cases (deaths plus those whose systems have recovered). This of course is highly impacted by measurement, and with coronavirus, mild cases may not even realize they have the disease, and in many cases, the count is dependent upon who is tested. Note that mortality is impacted by many factors, to include population density as well as the availability of treatment facility capacity and testing. The WHO fatality rate was estimated to be around 2%, compared to 10% for SARS and 34% for MERS. According to the worldometers. info is estimated by the WHO, the contagion rate for COVID-19 was found to be between 1.4 and 2.5, where a number below 1 would gradually disappear. Common flu has a rate of 1.3 and SARS had a rate of 2.0. But clearly COVID-19 is much more rapidly spread, while having less impact in terms of deaths per case.

2.4   Measures

Governments and health agencies have developed procedures to control epidemics. Bell and Lewis [3] reviewed prevention measures adopted to counteract the spread of four of the diseases covered (see Table 2.2).

Kanof [4] reviewed measures that worked in controlling SARS in the US. These measures included:

- Case identification through screening those with fever, cough, and recent travel to countries with known active cases of SARS.
- Contact tracing to identify and track those who had close contact with suspected infected individuals.
- Transmission control measures such as hand washing after contact, protection against respiratory spread, the use of isolation rooms with controlled airflow, and use of respiratory masks by health care workers.
- Exposure management through isolation and quarantine in health care and home settings.

In the Taiwan SARS outbreak, medical authorities adopted five guidelines:

1. Full quarantine measures.
2. A SARS task force was established to include medical and governmental officials.
3. Government agencies provided twice-daily updates to calm public fears.
4. Regular reports were given to foreign representatives about the latest SARS developments.
5. Relief funds were provided to industries including tourism, transportation, and recreation.

Table 2.2 Prevention measures adopted

Disease	Time	Transmission	Nature	Preventive measures
Bubonic plague	Fourteenth century	Respiratory	Bubos—Death in 3–4 days	Isolation
			Mortality: 60–70%	Rat control
Influenza	1918–1919	Aerosol	Within 48 h	Isolation
			Death in a few days	Quarantine
				Hygiene
				Vaccination
HIV/AIDS	1980s– current	Blood, sexual	8–10 year delay	Prevent bodily fluid contact
			Death average 7 years from diagnosis	
SARS	2002/2003	Respiratory	Symptoms in 4–5 days	Isolation
			Death possible within 48 h	Quarantine
			Mortality: 10–15%	Hygiene

Prager et al. [5] studied the impact of vaccination for influenza in the United States. They estimated that without avoidance efforts, an influenza outbreak could result in a loss of over $25 billion to US GDP from a reduction in workforce participation and an increase in medical expenditures. They argued that vaccination could reduce this to below $20 billion. These estimates rose substantially if avoidance behavior (stay at home; children kept from school; reduction in travel) and economic resilience in the form of production recovery from overtime or extra shifts were included.

The site www.worldmeters.info gives the following measures undertaken by the Italian authorities:

Sixteen days after the onset of the outbreak in Italy, much of Northern Italy was placed under a lockdown, consisting of:

- Travel in and out of the area restricted to verified professional requirements, emergency situations, or for health reasons.
- Those with symptoms and fever encouraged to stay home and to contact their doctor.
- All schools and universities were closed.
- All museums and cultural sites were closed.
- All religious, cultural, and festive events were suspended.
- Cinemas, pubs, theaters, casinos, nightclubs, and similar gathering places were closed.
- All sporting events and competitions were suspended.
- Bars and restaurants were allowed to open between 8 a.m. and 6 p.m. provided a safety distance of at least 1 m between customers was maintained.
- Shopping centers and department stores were closed on public holidays and the days preceding them.
- Places of worship remained open, given that a safety distance of 1 m was maintained—but ceremonies to include marriage and baptism were prohibited until further notice.

Nationally less restrictive conditions were imposed.

Comparisons of these different global epidemics would appear to call for government action, which to date has taken the form of quarantine, funding for increasing supplies of masks and test kits, and initial research for an antivirus. Meanwhile, there has been a significant impact on global supply chains and a consequent impact on the global economy. Leaner supply chains expose more severe disruption because they are longer, larger, and more complex.

2.5 Chinese Experience

Since the outbreak of the pandemic, China has quickly constructed a comprehensive multilevel grid-like pandemic prevention and control system. The Chinese government cooperates with medical care and the general public, implements a scientific and precise prevention and control strategy, and uses information technology such as big data, e-commerce and Health Codes system, takes the community as one of the most important lines of defence, adopts the principles of "early detection, early reporting, early isolation, early treatment," and carries out measures, including isolation, quarantine, hygiene, and coordinating the deployment of medical resources, etc. The stringent measures in Hubei Province helped to suppress the spread of the pandemic to other areas of China. A report by WHO pointed out that China has accumulated important experience in the prevention and control of the pandemic, especially adopting public health measures suitable for different regions according to local conditions, and effectively controlled the spread of the pandemic [6].

While strengthening the prevention and control of the pandemic, the Chinese government has implemented stable and flexible monetary policies and active and loose fiscal policies to vigorously support the real economy, especially small and medium-sized enterprises (SMEs), work and production resuming at a faster pace. The emerging service industry had a good growth momentum in the first quarter, where the added value of the service sector of information transmission, software and information technology and the financial sector increased by 13.2% and 6.0%, respectively [7]. Examination of the Chinese experience of the coronavirus experience relative to supply chains has found that the pandemic accelerated e-commerce and centralization of the fresh food industry, accelerating the catering model in the food sector. With the help of the "contactless distribution" service, fresh food e-commerce has gained economic progress and become the preferred lifestyle of "stay-at-home" citizens and also become an important channel for the upward trend of agricultural products to be sold. A variety of farmers and agricultural enterprises make use of large platforms such as Taobao and Jingdong and carry out community group purchase or open live broadcast to realize from slow selling to direct selling. In addition, the pandemic has brought opportunities for the transformation and upgrading of the manufacturing industry. For example, Baosteel Corporation uses "non-face-to-face manufacturing," "smart logistics," and other intelligent methods to ensure coronavirus prevention and control, and achieve efficient production operations as well. Moreover, block chain technology has been successfully applied to the field of supply chain finance. On February 7, the credit and debt platform of supply chain based on block chain in Beijing was officially launched. This platform realizes the right to confirm accounts receivable of government and state-owned enterprises' procurement contracts through the block chain underlying technology, and aggregates various financial resources such as financing guarantee and asset management to provide a full range of supply chain financial services for SMEs.

2.6 Conclusions

Today's social and economic development is highly correlated to health risk analytics issues such as the spread of epidemic diseases. Supply chain risk management tools for pandemics include reduction of threats through strong health provision, while mitigation is fostered through real-time monitoring. The experience across countries in the world seems to provide a metric of the strength of health care systems. Real-time monitoring has been challenging as any new strain would cause. But the rapid spread characteristic of the virus imposes quite a threat to areas of the world in the early stages of exposure, such as Africa and South America.

Supply chains have evolved, based on the responses to previous risk situations by becoming more agile, more robust, more redundant, as appropriate for each organization and each risk occurrence. This will clearly continue as new situations occur, with the trend to create more complex systems seeking optimality, thus creating more risk. It is important for all organizations to be prepared to react to new information as it becomes available, but identifying links between these new situations and previous experience will serve organizations well in evaluating immediate reactions.

As supply chains adapt to these new conditions, we see a significant short-term impact on the economy as cargo ships can't process through ports, commercial air traffic, and cruise ship travel drop considerably, and so forth. These changes affect organizations and individuals in a significant way in the short term and some may never fully recover. We see an immediate impact with headlines like "World Economy Shudders as Coronavirus Threatens Global Supply Chains" (Wall Street Journal—WSJ, February 23, 2020), "Global Economy Shows Strain as Virus Starts to Take a Toll" (WSJ, February 24, 2020), and "U.S. Stocks Climb Following Monday Selloff" (WSJ, February 25, 2020) as investors react, overreact, and then calm down. The Chinese experience has seen further increase in the emerging service industry of the service sector of information transmission, software and information technology, and the financial sector such as fresh food e-commerce markets and supply chain finance based on block chain technology. There also has been growth in the food catering industry. Supply chain members in all categories will see opportunities to gain advantages from production capacity, warehousing, and logistics capabilities. Part of the adaptation process would seem to be an acceleration in automation, replacing human labor with technology. Expanded use of customer demand data mining will be needed to keep on top of changes in demands. The coronavirus experience will accelerate this change in business models for supply chains.

By the time of publication, possibly the world economy will collapse—but we feel it far more likely that it will recover in a more economically robust form. Meanwhile, many humans will have to find new means of employment. We also feel that the coronavirus will continue to spread throughout the world, but like other flu, the vast majority of the population will survive.

Ultimately, as supply chains evolve and recover through these threats, we will continue to uncover ongoing evolution of processes and infrastructures. Ultimately, after some initial shaking out of the supply chains, we will see most move into a long-term recovery mode, potentially with new opportunities that will strengthen them over time and provide insight for future improvement.

References

1. Ginsberg, J., Mohebbi, M. H., Patel, R. S. A., Brammer, L., Smolinski, M. S., & Brilliant, L. (2009). Detecting influenza epidemics using search engine query data. *Nature, 457*(7232), 1012–1014.
2. Feldman, B., Martin, E.M., & Skotnes, T. (2012). *Big data in healthcare hype and hope* (Dr. Bonnie 360: Business Development for Digital Health, pp. 122–125).
3. Bell, C., & Lewis, M. (2004). The economic implications of epidemics old and new. *World Economics, 5*(4), 137–174.
4. Kanof, M.E. (2003). *Severe acute respiratory syndrome: Established infectious disease control measures helped contain spread, but a large-scale resurgence may pose challenges* (United States General Accounting Office GAO-03-1058T) (pp. 1–20).
5. Prager, F., Wei, D., & Rose, A. (2017). Total economic consequences of an influenza outbreak in the United States. *Risk Analysis, 37*(1), 4–19.
6. Coronavirus Disease 2019 (COVID-19). Situation report-76. https://www.who.int/docs/default-source/coronaviruse/situation-reports/20200405-sitrep-76-COVID-19.pdf?sfvrsn=6ecf0977_4
7. http://www.stats.gov.cn/tjsj/zxfb/202004/t20200417_1739327.html

Chapter 3
System Dynamics Modeling of Contagion Effects

Abstract Financial contagion has been with us as long as there has been an economy. The system of collective human behavior usually creates stable markets, but occasionally, this collective behavior results in various bubbles. Financial contagion specifically deals with the domino effect of one banking institution failure, which, due to interrelationships with other banks, leads to further failures. A decision support model of accounts receivable risk management is presented. Financial contagion and bubbles are discussed. The year 1929 was a very bad year, but 2008 had its moments as well. These financial contagions result in undermining confidence in similar institutions. Our research question is to examine the role of accounts receivable payments that are affected by the social interaction of those holding loans from a lending institution. System dynamics modeling is used to demonstrate the impact of word-of-mouth social contacts on accounts receivable and the ensuing increase in financial risk. This was proposed as a decision support tool for a common banking risk-management problem: Accounts Receivable risk management.

The traumatic financial events based on real estate derivatives in 2008 have had a major impact on risk management. Social interaction can have both positive and negative effects on the repayment of loans. The spread of rumors and new ideas, firm financial performance, and repaid loans can all have positive or negative feedback, which can be viewed as a spread of infection of those who have not repaid. As early payers of an account expose their friends, families, acquaintances, and colleagues to their experiences, some are persuaded to change their beliefs concerning firm performance. This can, in turn, influence subsequent repayment behavior of those which whom those who repay their loans share information.

The turmoil in the United States financial markets and the subsequent financial crisis was attributable to financial contagion. This paper develops a system dynamics

---

This chapter is drawn from D. Wu and D.L. Olson, A System Dynamics Modeling of Contagion Effects in Accounts Risk Management, Systems Research and Behavioral Science 31(4), 502–511, with permission.

D. D. Wu, D. L. Olson, *Pandemic Risk Management in Operations and Finance*,
Computational Risk Management, https://doi.org/10.1007/978-3-030-52197-4_3

19

model of financial contagion at the operational level. Our research question is: "How are accounts receivable payments to a lending institution affected by the social interaction of those holding loans?"

3.1 Financial Contagion

Bubbles have been endemic in human practice, beginning with the Dutch tulip mania in the early seventeenth century and early real estate investment opportunities such as the South Sea Company (1711–1720) and the Mississippi Company (1719–1720). Isaac Newton was considered one of the smartest people in the world but lost heavily in such bubbles. He is credited with stating, "I can calculate the motion of heavenly bodies but not the madness of people." You might think that we have learned to control investment bubbles, but the London Market Exchange experienced a spiral in 1983 when excess-of-loss reinsurance became popular, and syndicates ended up paying themselves to insure themselves against ruin. These syndicates viewed risks as independent. They did not realize that they were hedging against themselves. In 1983, Hurricane Alicia caused heavy claims that brought this system down and early supply chain-related bubble. An example of a model gone mad was the use of the Black-Scholes model to price derivatives on the part of Long-Term Capital Management (LTCM) [1]. They ended up viewing risk with return and invested in Russian banks, which tumbled in the 1990s, bringing down LCTM with them. There was also a dot-com bubble in the early year or two of the twenty-first Century, following madness on the part of venture capitalists seeking anything to do with e-business sites. We all are far too familiar with the 2008 bubble in CDOs, still impacting Europe.

Well-developed economic theory assumes a tendency toward equilibrium. Alternative economic views have been presented by Nassim Taleb [2], who presented the Black Swan problem. Humans try to be scientific and learn from their observations and history. But while nobody in Europe had seen a black swan and had thus assumed that they did not exist, when they settled in Australia, they found some, disproving their empirical hypothesis. Taleb also points to fallacies on the part of investors, who assume that data are normally distributed. A bubble is a large, long-term drop in asset price, be it stocks, bonds, or houses. Bubbles typically come from human expectations of exaggerated or unwarranted favorable trends. In practice, especially during bubble bursts, fat tails with higher extreme probabilities are often observed. Cognitive psychology can explain some of this. Kahneman and Tversky [3] emphasized human biases from framing, with different attitudes toward risk found during winning and losing streaks. Humans have also been found to overestimate the probability of rare events, such as the odds of the next asteroid impacting the earth or the risk of terrorists on airplanes. Akerlof and Shiller [4] argued that standard economic theory makes too many assumptions. When human decisions are involved, historical data are not a good predictor of future performance.

3.2 System Dynamics Tools

System dynamics was developed by Jay Forrester [5] and others. It has its roots in general systems theory from the 1930s [6] and the work on cybernetic systems including that of Stafford Beer [7]. Open systems theory views organizations relative to their environments, with a continuous flow of information between the organization and the environment. System dynamics models can reflect the interaction among dynamic markets, uncertain production systems, and cash flow features of operating businesses. Cybernetic systems are complex, probabilistic, and purposive, with feedback and control. This feedback and control is a characteristic of system dynamic simulation models. Sterman [8] has been especially active in publishing accounts of the application of system dynamics in academic research.

System dynamic models have been used to study financial contagion [9]. System dynamics allows consideration of a number of factors, to include word of mouth. Quality of service has become a critical factor in today's consumer society. Service businesses face a decision concerning the tradeoff between expenditures to increase quality and loss of business from failure to do so. Not only are unsatisfied customers unlikely to return, but they are also a prime source of negative influence on potential customers.

Archer and Wesolowsky [10] gave a word-of-mouth model for a service business with a pool of existing clients who conduct business with the firm. A certain proportion of clients is dissatisfied with their service. The firm attracts new customers from the public at a given rate. They used a Markov model with a growing number of customers drawn into the system from advertising. Positive experiences have an influence on attracting new customers, while negative experiences dampen business. System dynamics models can include a variety of feedback mechanisms over time. We began with a simple model considering the impact of word of mouth on generated business.

3.3 Accounts Receivable Data and Model

As the global economy entered a new era after the crisis of 2008, business models and assumptions need a review. Financial operation professionals should today consider dependence and contagion among multisource data and risk factors, whether the risk involves credit, markets, operations, or enterprise risk aggregation. Figure 3.1 demonstrates the number of accounts receivable for eight giant companies from 1993-12-1 to 2014-1-31. It can be seen from the figure that the amount of accounts receivable for most companies jumps to a higher level. Moreover, this higher level of accounts receivable amount keeps a long time. For example, this very high amount has not decreased for Microsoft Corporation (MSFT) much since the financial crisis in late 2007. It has been constantly increasing for Apple Inc. (AAPL).

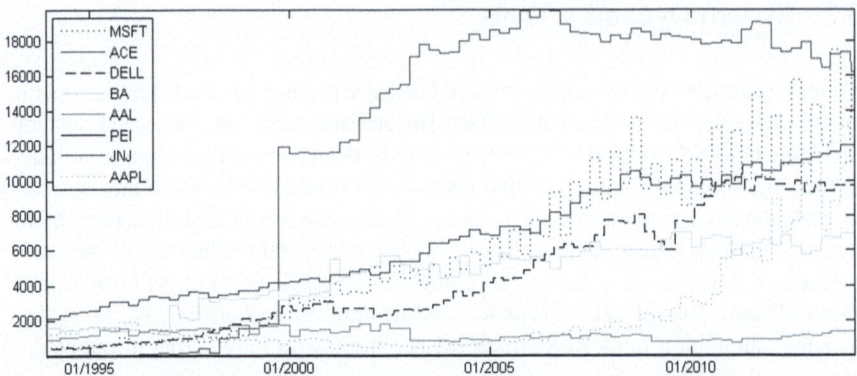

Fig. 3.1 Accounts receivable for eight large companies from 1993-12-1 to 2014-1-31

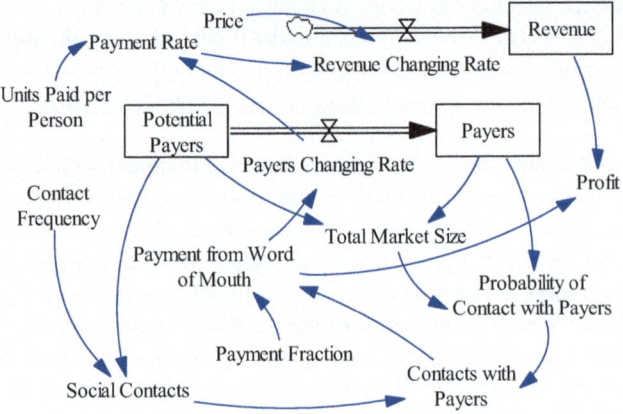

Fig. 3.2 System dynamics model of contagion effects used in the study

Consider the growth of accounts payment for a firm. This time series usually grows exponentially initially, but then as the market begins to saturate, growth slows until the series hits an upper bound determined by the size of the potential market for the product category. The decision support system that we propose relies on the development and application of standard system dynamics models for sensitivity analysis and prediction using standard system dynamics software.

3.3.1   System Dynamics Model

Figure 3.2 demonstrates the contagion structure of a simple accounts payment model using system dynamics. The total market for accounts is divided into two types: those who have already paid (the Payers) and those who have not yet paid (the

Potential payers). As people pay their accounts, the Payer Changing Rate rises, moving people from the Potential payers' pool to the payers' pool. In this system dynamics model, we assume that payment occurs only through word of mouth, that is, Payers' Changing Rate is equal to Payment from Word of Mouth. Potential payers keep in contact with payers through social interactions. The firm owning all accounts may invest in a platform to facilitate social interactions if the firm can benefit from such social interactions. Naturally, not all potential payers are infected through interaction with payers. The persuasiveness of the word of mouth and the confidence in the firm affect the fraction of word of mouth encounters that result in payment of the accounts. The Payment Fraction is the probability that a given interaction or contagion between a payer and potential payer results in payment by the potential payer.

Potential payers come into contact with payers through social interactions. A fraction of these contacts result in likely payment of the accounts owned as a result of favorable word of mouth. Revenue is given by the price and payment rate; payment equals the payers' changing rate times the number of units paid by each payer. The model assumes no aftermarket revenues.

3.3.2 Firm Performance

In the Vensim software, we set the following equations for the stock and flow structure:

$$\text{Payers} = \text{INTEG}(\text{Payment Rate}, \text{Initial Payers}), \tag{3.1}$$

$$\text{Potential Payers} = \text{INTEG}(-\text{Payment Rate}, \text{Total Market Size} - \text{Payers}). \tag{3.2}$$

We assume that the payment time period is in the unit of month. People owning to the firm are assumed to interact with each other at some rate. Contact Frequency is the number of other people, with each person owning to the firm, comes in contact with, on average, per month. Therefore, the Contacts with Payers experienced by all potential Payers per month is

$$
\begin{aligned}
\text{Contacts with Payers} &= \text{Social Contacts} \\
&\quad * \text{Probability of Contact with Payers} \\
&= \text{Contact Frequency} * \text{Potential Payers} \\
&\quad * \text{Probability of Contact with Payers}.
\end{aligned} \tag{3.3}
$$

We assume that the initial value of both Potential Payers and Payers is 50,000. To make comparisons, we set the following five conditions:

Condition 1: Contact Frequency $= 1$, Payment Fraction $= 1$, Units Paid per Person $= 1$, Price $= 1$

Condition 2: Contact Frequency = 0.5, Payment Fraction = 1, Units Paid per Person = 1, Price = 1
Condition 3:Contact Frequency = 1, Payment Fraction = 2,Units Paid per Person = 1, Price = 1
Condition 4: Contact Frequency = 1, Payment Fraction = 1, Units Paid per Person = 0.5, Price = 1
Condition 5: Contact Frequency = 1, Payment Fraction = 1, Units Paid per Person = 1, Price = 2

The essence is that Condition 1 is the base case, Condition 2 reduces contact frequency, Condition 3 doubles payment fraction, Condition 4 reduces units paid per person to half, and Condition 5 doubles price. Each provides an opportunity to study the expected impact of one change in the basic model.

3.4   Results and Discussion

We ran this system dynamics model using Vensim software. The dynamics are shown in Figs. 3.3 (revenue), 3.4 (profit), and 3.5 (population trends). Firm performance is demonstrated using both revenue and profit. Profit is equal to revenue minus the cost incurred by investing in social contacts. We assume that the cost is a quadratic function of social contacts. For all five cases, both revenue and profit grow during the first stages as potential payers migrate to payers, but then as the market begins to saturate, it hits an upper bound determined by the size of the market for the accounts owned by the firm. Firm revenue reaches the maximum earlier than the profit in all cases.

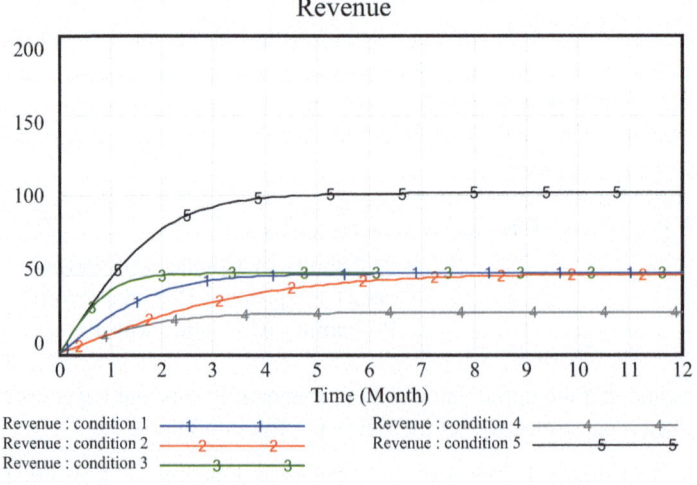

Fig. 3.3 Dynamics of firm revenue

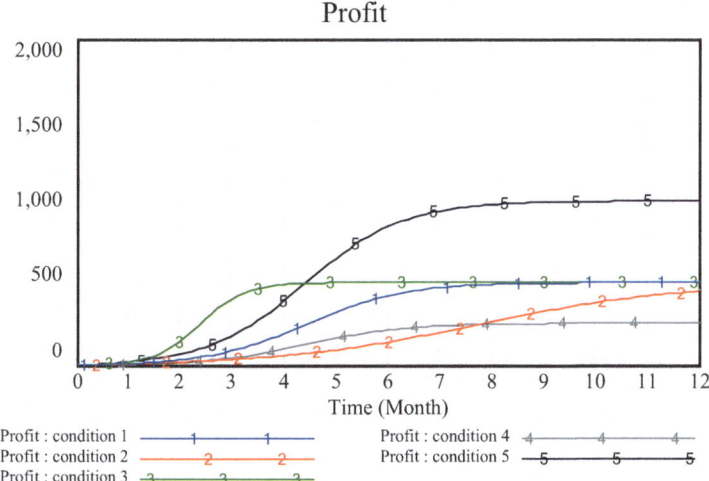

Fig. 3.4 Dynamics of firm profit

Contact Frequency value in Condition 1 is unity, while Contact Frequency value in Condition 2 is 0.5. Therefore, it is observed from both Figs. 3.3 and 3.4 that a more frequent social contact leads to higher revenue and profit. Meanwhile, a higher social Contact Frequency yields higher payer size moved from potential payers, as can be observed in Fig. 3.5.

With respect to revenue, doubling the payment fraction (Condition 3) can be seen to have a quicker increase in revenue and reducing contact frequency has a slower initial revenue increase, but both reach the basic model level by month 7. Reducing units paid per person has a more permanent reduction in revenue, while increased price with no interaction effects leads to the doubling of revenues.

With respect to profit, doubling the payment fraction (Condition 3) can be seen to have a quicker positive response that stabilizes to the base case by month 7. Reducing contact frequency (Condition 2) has a slower initial revenue increase but approaches the basic model level by month 12. Reducing units paid per person (Condition 4) has a more permanent reduction in revenue, while increased price with no interaction effects leads to the doubling of profit.

With respect to population trends, doubling the payment fraction (Condition 3) can be seen to quickly reduce the pool of Potential Payers by increasing the proportion of Payers. Reducing contact frequency (Condition 2) has the reverse effect. The changes associated with Conditions 4 and 5 have no discernable effect on the basic model payer pools.

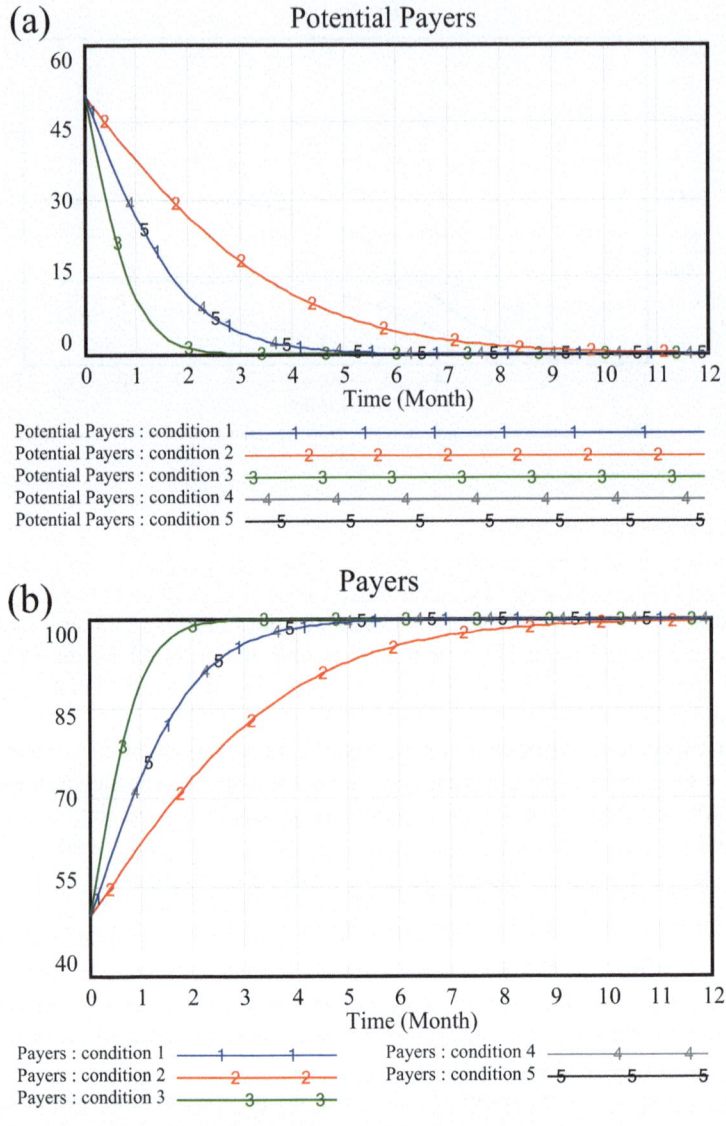

Fig. 3.5 Population trends. (**a**) Potential payers and (**b**) payers

3.4.1   Social Interaction

This section explores the effect of social contacts on firm performance by adjusting the contagion intensity in the model. Social contacts from the model are shown in Fig. 3.6:

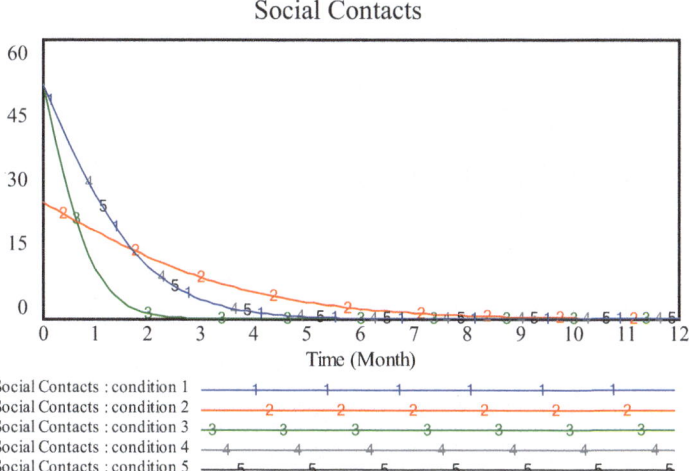

Fig. 3.6 Dynamics of social contacts

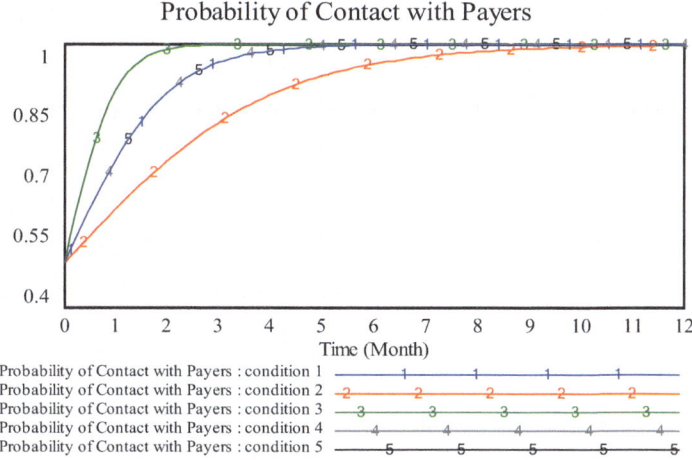

Fig. 3.7 Dynamics of probability of contact with payers

As can be seen in Fig. 3.7, Probability of Contact with Payers converges to unity faster in Condition 1 than in Condition 2 since the Contact Frequency value in Condition is higher than that in Condition 2. Condition 3 is again the inverse of Condition 2. However, the dynamics of social contacts in Fig. 3.6 suggests that the number of social contacts is higher in Condition 1 when the Contact Frequency value is higher in around a month and 20 days while lower than that in Condition 2 after that. Correspondingly, both the Payment from Word of Mouth and payment rate show a similar pattern, as can be observed in Figs. 3.8 and 3.9.

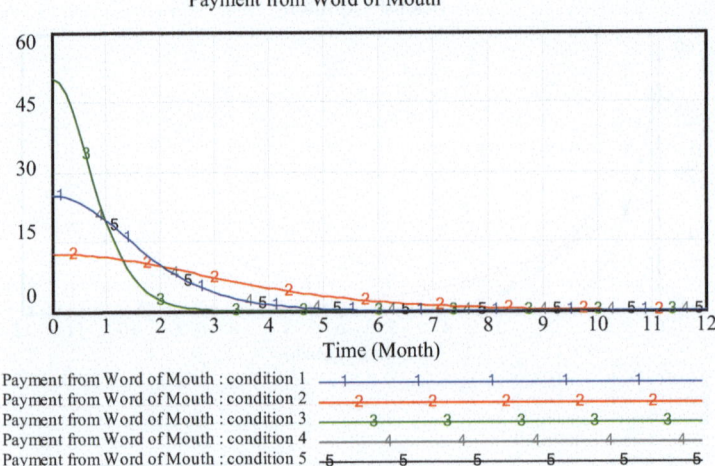

Fig. 3.8 Dynamics of payment from word of mouth

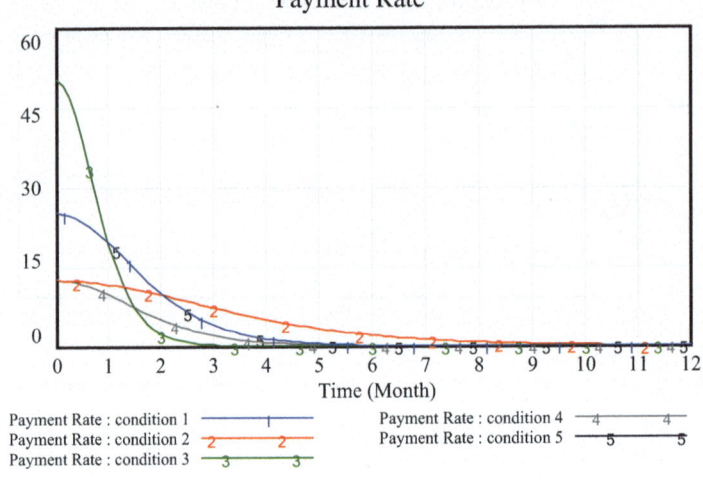

Fig. 3.9 Dynamics of payment rate

Social contagion continues until the population of potential payers has been depleted some months later (e.g., around 5 months later for both the first and fourth cases), and the payment rate falls to zero.

3.5 Conclusions

Vensim PLE software is a standard academic system dynamics software. It is an excellent tool enabling the use of objects to support features such as arrays, automated calibration, optimization, sensitivity analysis, data linking, and so on. It, thus, serves as an excellent decision support system.

The essential differences identified in our system dynamics model are that reducing units paid per person while holding all else equal (Condition 4) has the reverse effect on revenue and profit of doubling price (Condition 5), while changes modeled in contact frequency (Condition 2) and payment fraction (Condition 3) converged to the basic model after a period of 6 or 7 months. Conditions 2 and 3 had an inverse impact with respect to the pools of Potential Payers and Payers, as well as Social Contacts and Probability of Contact. Conditions 2 and 3 also had an inverse impact on Payment from Word of Mouth as well as Payment Rate.

Accounts receivable involve financial risk, which was recognized as critically important after scandals and market disruptions centering around 2000, and has become even more critical since 2008. Accurate management of risk enables firms to profit, even in turbulent markets.

References

1. Lowenstein, R. (2000). *When genius failed: The rise and fall of long-term capital management.* New York: Random House.
2. Taleb, N. N. (2007). *The black swan: The impact of the highly improbable.* London: Penguin Books.
3. Kahneman, D., & Tversky, A. (1979). Prospect theory: An analysis of decision under risk. *Econometrica, 47*(2), 263–292.
4. Akerlof, G. A., & Shiller, R. J. (2009). *Animal spirits: How human psychology drives the economy, and why it matters for global capitalism.* Princeton, NJ: Princeton University Press.
5. Forrester, J. W. (1961). *Industrial dynamics.* New York, NY: Wiley.
6. Von Bertalanffy, L. (1968). *General system theory: Foundations, development, applications.* New York: George Braziller.
7. Beer, S. (1967). *Brain of the firm.* United Kingdom: Penguin Press.
8. Sterman, J. D., Repenning, N. P., & Kofman, F. (1997). Unanticipated side effects of successful quality programs: Exploring a paradox of organizational improvement. *Management Science, 43*(4), 503–521.
9. Harvey, J. T. (2002). Keynes' chapter 22: A system dynamics model. *Journal of Economic Issues, 36*(2), 373–381.
10. Archer, N. P., & Wesolowsky, G. O. (1994). A dynamic service quality cost model with world-of-mouth advertising. *European Journal of Operational Research, 78*, 355–366.

Chapter 4
Text Mining Support to Pandemic Planning

Abstract Text mining is a useful tool to identify sentiment. Not only it is widely used in stock market operations but it can also be applied to analyze Web content or other documents related to pandemic operations. A support vector machine is a data mining algorithm useful for certain types of data. This chapter demonstrates the use of a Web crawler to identify financial sentiment, a process that would also work for pandemic management. A support vector model is applied to a Chinese stock market index, demonstrating that technology also could be extended to pandemic planning and control.

4.1 Text Mining of Financial Data

An example application of text mining and sentiment analysis is to identify stock market trends, a challenging but useful task. Stock market indices are nonlinear and dynamic, and investor sentiment constitutes a key factor of the financial market. With the proliferation of news, blogs, forums, and social networking websites, textual content on the Internet provides a precious source to reflect investor sentiment and predicts stock prices as a complement to traditional stock market time series data. Hence, an automated approach is required to distill knowledge from a large number of textual documents. Sentiment analysis is used to automatically extract views, attitudes, and emotions from the opinionated contents [1]. Sentiment analysis is demonstrated in this chapter by constructing sentiment indices, which are then aggregated with stock market data to forecast movement direction. This application could be extended to hospital bed demand planning in the pandemic management environment.

In order to get an efficient and persuasive sentiment index, day-of-week effects can be important. The average return on Mondays is much lower than that on the

---

This chapter is taken from a paper by Ren, R., Wu, D. and Liu, T. (2017). Forecasting stock market movement direction using sentiment analysis and support vector machine. *IEEE Systems Journal* 13(1), 760–770 with permission.

D. D. Wu, D. L. Olson, *Pandemic Risk Management in Operations and Finance*,
Computational Risk Management, https://doi.org/10.1007/978-3-030-52197-4_4

other days of the week. It is one of the most well-known financial anomalies dating back to 1930 when Fred C. Kelly revealed the phenomenon on the US markets where the returns had the tendency to decline on Mondays [2]. Day-of-week effect is seldom mentioned when it comes to calculating sentiment indices.

Another difficulty in predicting stock movement direction is attributed to its nonlinear, dynamic, and evolutionary properties. Support Vector Machine (SVM) has been widely utilized since it can solve the nonlinear problem by converting it to a quadratic programming. Moreover, the solution of an SVM is unique and globally optimal [3]. It can also reduce the overfitting problem by selecting the maximal margin hyperplane in the feature space [4]. To further address the problem, in this demonstration, five-fold cross-validation is applied. This leads to look-ahead bias, and so, the SVM model is integrated with a realistic rolling window approach to eliminate that bias. Empirical results illustrate that combining sentiment features with stock market data outperforms using only stock market data in forecasting movement direction. The results indicate that investor sentiment plays an important role in the stock market. Furthermore, a sentiment probably contains precious information about the asset fundamental values and can be regarded as one of the leading indicators of the stock market.

The prediction results also imply trade order: 1 means buy order, whereas -1 means sell order. Thus, investor behavior when investment decisions are solely based on the results in a real market environment can be modeled. It is assumed that short selling is allowed and that there are no market frictions. By integrating sentiment indices to the basic model, investors can make more profit and, at the same time, bear less risk. In addition, a stop loss order strategy is applied to limit the potential losses, improving performance a great deal.

The purpose is to forecast the stock market movement direction not only by using financial market data but also by combining them with sentiment features that incorporate investor psychology. The features are extracted from unstructured news data automatically and then are expressed as sentiment indices. In order to make the indices more realistic and reliable, the day-of-week effect is considered. SVM is then applied to forecast stock market trends using a rolling window approach, which is compared with the baseline method. Prediction results are used to instruct investment decisions, and the performance of three different trading strategies is evaluated and compared.

4.2 Investor Sentiment

The first step is to construct a web crawler to download news documents automatically from the Internet and then construct daily sentiment indices based on the corpus. Adjustments are made to consider the day-of-week effect.

Step 1: Web crawler

The web crawler automatically downloads textual documents from the Internet and stores them in a database for further processing. The web crawler begins with the seeds in the form of a list of URLs. The scheduler manages the queue of URLs, deciding the priority and eliminating duplicate parts. Next, the downloader is responsible for acquiring the web pages from the Internet and providing them to the spider, which is used to parse the pages and extract the targeted contents. Two types of data are needed: one is the textual news with the date from the websites, stored with previous data into the database, and the other is the URLs contained in the pages, which are transported to the Scheduler. Procedures are repeated until all targeted textual documents are obtained. Each document can be displayed by time, headline, and contents.

Step 2: Daily sentiment

A sentence-based sentiment analysis approach is used to process the textual data during a specific period. A sentence is a unit to interpret the meaning of the whole document instead of a single word because a sentence can express a relatively complete meaning and help address the ambiguity problem. As a result, a document is first divided into sentences. Next, sentences are segmented into separate words, with words projected onto the sentiment space. The number of positive and negative words is counted, specific sentiment values are assigned, and polarity of each sentence is determined based on HowNet and the Chinese Sentiment Analysis Ontology Base. HowNet is an online commonsense knowledge base unveiling interconceptual relationships and interattribute relationships of concepts as connoted in lexicons of the Chinese and their English equivalents. The Chinese Sentiment Analysis Ontology Base is constructed by the Dalian University of Technology and depicts words and phrases from various aspects containing parts of speech, polarity, and sentiment intensity. After that, each document is categorized. As there may be a large number of posts or articles in a day, a daily sentiment index S_t is calculated using (4.1),

$$S_t = \begin{cases} 2M_t^{\text{bull}}/\left(M_t^{\text{bull}} + M_t^{\text{bear}}\right) - 1, & M_t^{\text{bull}} > M_t^{\text{bear}} \\ 0, & M_t^{\text{bull}} = M_t^{\text{bear}} \\ 1 - 2M_t^{\text{bear}}/\left(M_t^{\text{bull}} + M_t^{\text{bear}}\right), & M_t^{\text{bull}} < M_t^{\text{bear}} \end{cases}, \qquad (4.1)$$

where M_t^{bull} denotes the number of positive comments, whereas M_t^{bear} denotes the number of negative comments in day t. The value of S_t ranges from -1 to 1, where 0 means that people hold a neutral position. If the value is larger than 0, it means that most people take a positive view; if the value is less than 0, it means that most people take a negative view.

Step 3: Sentiment modification

The day-of-week effect is one of the most well-known financial anomalies. The average return on a Monday is much lower than that on the other days of the week. In part, this is because a large amount of news is reported on the weekend or on Friday just after the market is closed. With such considerable and valuable information to deal with, investors are very likely to change their mind and take actions on Mondays. Furthermore, corporations tend to release important news on the weekend to ensure the stability of the stock and boost their public image. If it is bad news, investors will have enough time to digest and accept it, whereas if it is good news, companies can continuously spread out news to make it known by more and more people and expand their coverage.

In this procedure, the effect from Saturday to Monday is modeled through an exponential time function as news has a greater impact when it is more recent. Sentiment can be modeled with an exponential function of past price changes on the stock market. Here, sentiment on Monday is modeled as a weighted average of past sentiment where the weights decrease exponentially. The expression is clarified in (4.2),

$$S_m = e^{-\lambda t_1} S_1 + e^{-\lambda t_2} S_2 + e^{-\lambda t_3} S_3, \tag{4.2}$$

where S_1, S_2, and S_3 stand for the Saturday sentiment, Sunday sentiment, and Monday sentiment, respectively; S_m is the modified Monday sentiment; $\lambda(\lambda > 0)$ is prescribed; $t_1 = 2$, $t_2 = 1$, and $t_3 = 0$.

Similarly, the stock market is also closed on national holidays or on some special days, and so, activities on such days are generalized (4.2) to more common occasions. Assume that there are n holiday days on the stock market, and then, the sentiment on the $n + 1$ day is represented in (4.3),

$$S_{n+1} = e^{-n\lambda} S_1 + e^{-(n-1)\lambda} S_2 + \cdots + e^{-\lambda} S_n + S_{n+1}. \tag{4.3}$$

4.3 Support Vector Machines

Support vector machine (SVM) is a supervised machine learning model for classification [5]. Assume that there is an input space X, an output space Y, and a training dataset T,

$$T = \{(x_i, y_i), i = 1, \cdots, l\} \in (X \times Y)^l, \tag{4.4}$$

where $x_i \in R^n$ and $y_i \in Y = \{-1, 1\}$, then, introduce a transformation $x = f(x)$ such that $R^n \rightarrow H$, in which H is the Hilbert space, and so, the training set is then given by (4.5),

$$T_f = \{(x_i, y_i), i = 1, \cdots, l\} \in (H \times Y)^l, \tag{4.5}$$

where $x_i = f(x_i) \in H$ and $y_i \in Y = \{-1, 1\}$. Thus, we can find a linear separating hyperplane $(w^* \cdot x) + b^* = 0$ in the Hilbert space, and then, we can obtain a separating hyperplane $w^* \cdot f(x) + b^* = 0$ and a decision function $D(x) = \text{sgn}((w^* \cdot x) + b^*) = \text{sgn}(w^* \cdot f(x) + b^*)$ in the original space R^n.

SVM is an optimization problem, which aims to maximize the margin. The margin between two hyperplanes in the Hilbert space is $2/\|w\|$. The two hyperplanes are classified in (4.6),

$$(w \cdot x) + b = 1 \text{ and } (w \cdot x) + b = -1. \tag{4.6}$$

SVM model can be represented as

$$\min_{\omega, b, \xi} \quad \frac{1}{2}\|w\|^2 + C\sum_{i=1}^{l}\xi_i, \tag{4.7}$$

$$\text{s.t. } y_i((w \cdot f(x_i)) + b) \geq 1 - \xi_i, i = 1, \tag{4.8}$$

$$\xi_i \geq 0, i = 1, \cdots l, \tag{4.9}$$

where ξ_i is a tolerable training error and C is a positive constant parameter to evaluate the trade-off between training errors and margin maximization. In order to solve the problem, we can transform it to its dual problem, and the solution set of dual problems is the same as the QP problem, as shown in

$$\min_{\alpha} \quad \frac{1}{2}\sum_{i=1}^{l}\sum_{j=1}^{l}y_i y_j \alpha_i \alpha_j \left(f(x_i) \cdot f(x_j) \right) - \sum_{j=1}^{l}\alpha_j, \tag{4.10}$$

$$= \frac{1}{2}\sum_{i=1}^{l}\sum_{j=1}^{l}y_i y_j \alpha_i \alpha_j K(x_i, x_j) - \sum_{j=1}^{l}\alpha_j, \tag{4.11}$$

$$\text{s.t. } \sum_{i=1}^{l}y_i \alpha_i = 0, \tag{4.12}$$

$$0 \leq \alpha_i \leq C, i = 1, \cdots l, \tag{4.13}$$

where $\alpha = (\alpha_1, \cdots, \alpha_l)^T$ is a Lagrange multiplier; $K(x_i, x_j)$ is defined as a kernel function with $K(x_i, x_j) = (f(x_i) \cdot f(x_j))$, and $(\cdot)$ denotes the inner product in the Hilbert space. There are many kinds of kernel functions, such as RBF kernel $K_{rbf}(x_i, x_j) = \exp(-\gamma\|x_i - x_j\|^2)$ and polynomial kernel $K_{poly}(x_i, x_j) = ((x_i \cdot x_j) + 1)^d$, where γ, d are kernel parameters. Given parameter C and a proper kernel function $K(x_i, x_j)$, the solution $\alpha^* = (\alpha_1^*, \cdots, \alpha_l^*)^T$ of QP problem (4.11)–(4.13) can be identified, allowing calculation of b^*,

$$b^* = y_j - \sum_{i=1}^{l} y_i \alpha_i^* K(x_i, x_j).$$ (4.14)

Finally, decision function (4.15) is constructed to classify sentences,

$$D(x) = \text{sgn} \left(\sum_{i=1}^{l} y_i \alpha_i^* K(x_i, x_j) + b^* \right).$$ (4.15)

4.4 Experiment

This approach is demonstrated:

4.4.1 Data Description

The SSE 50 Index is a primarily blue-chip stock index on the Shanghai stock market, and it is made up of the 50 largest stocks of good liquidity and representativeness. The SSE 50 Index is modeled by using stock market data and exploiting news documents related to it and its constituents. Conventional time series data include opening price, closing price, high for the day, low for the day, trading volume in the number of shares, trading volume in RMB, change in RMB, and change in percentage. Data of the SSE 50 Index and its fifty constituents were downloaded from the Wind Economic Database, which is the market leader in China's financial information service industry.

A web crawler was built to download all the posts and documents of the 51 shares from the Sina stock forum and Eastmoney stock forum over the period of June 17th, 2014 and June seventh, 2016 including 485 trading days. The two forums are widely regarded as active and mainstream communities in China. The number of reviews of each stock is 37,855 on average, peaking at 23,236 and reaching the lowest point at 7797. The details are illustrated in the second column of Table 4.1. The total number of reviews on the Sina stock forum and Eastmoney stock forum is 1,930,592 after filtering and denoising during the given period.

4.4.2 Sentiment Calculation

Under Steps 2–3 above, 51 sentiment indices for the stocks in the study. In Step 2, each document was segmented into several sentences by identifying punctuations

Table 4.1 Description of features X1 to X8

Feature	Description
X1	Average of modified sentiment indices
X2	Highest of modified sentiment indices
X3	Lowest of modified sentiment indices
X4	Median of modified sentiment indices
X5	Value between the highest and the lowest
X6	Change in average
X7	Percentage of average change
X8	Standard deviation of modified sentiment indices

such as ',' '.,' and '!'. Then, sentences are divided into separate words, and if there appears a negative word, it is treated as a whole with the word next to it. For example, if people say '我不满意这股票 (I'm not satisfied with the stock)', after word segmentation, the sentence becomes four words '我(I'm)' '不(not)' '满意 (satisfied with)' '这(the)' '股票 (stock)'. If words are directly projected to the sentiment space, the program will identify if the sentence is optimistic because of the positive word '满意(satisfied with)' . So, treat '不(not)' and '满意(satisfied with)' as a whole '不满意 (not satisfied with)' to enable identification of true meaning. Then, each document is categorized. Assume that there are p_i positive sentences and n_i negative sentences in document i; if $p_i > n_i$, the document is positive; if $p_i = n_i$, the document is neutral; if $p_i < n_i$, the document is negative. This enables identification of knowledge such as on the day t, the number of positive comments is M_t^{bull} and the number of negative comments is M_t^{bear}, and so, a daily sentiment index is calculated by using formula (4.1), with the value ranging from -1 to 1, where 0 means that people hold a neutral position. If the value is between 0 and 1, it means that people hold a positive view; if the value is between -1 and 0, it means that people take a negative view. Then, by considering the day-of-week effect, the modified sentiment indices are calculated according to Eqs. (4.2) and (4.3).

The major statistics of the modified sentiment indices include the mean, median, standard deviation, skewness, and kurtosis of each stock sentiment index. This demonstrates that the majority of investors have a positive view on the fifty-one stocks since the mean and median of most stocks are positive rather than negative. The price of the SSE 50 Index increases at first and then drops suddenly, but overall, people are optimistic. This implies that people are not ready for the decrease. In fact, many individuals and companies lost a great deal during the period, which is also called the stock market disaster in China.

These are not utilized directly to explore the stock market trend. Eight sentiment indicators are based on fifty-one sentiment indices (Table 4.1). Reasons include that the number of features of market data and sentiment indices need to be balanced. Although we have already computed 51 sentiment indices, there are around ten items of market data, and so, it is unfair for the market attributes to some extent. Next, too many variables tend to cause the problem of overfitting. Furthermore, using eight sentiment features achieves a better result in forecasting the SSE 50 Index than using all fifty-one indices. Inspired by the market attributes, sentiment features consist of the highest of modified sentiment indices, the lowest of modified sentiment indices, the median of modified sentiment indices, the average of modified sentiment indices, the difference between the highest and the lowest, the change in the average (a certain day's average minus the last day's average), the percentage of the average change (a certain day's average minus the last day's average and divided by the last day's average), and the standard deviation of fifty-one modified sentiment indices.

4.4.3   Prediction

Data are labeled according to (4.16),

$$
Label = \begin{cases} 1, & Close_{t\text{-}1} < Close_t \\ -1, & Close_{t\text{-}1} > Close_t \end{cases}, \tag{4.16}
$$

where $Close_t$ denotes the close price of the SSE 50 Index and $Close_{t-1}$ stands for the close price on the previous day. Besides, 1 also means buy order as it indicates the increase, whereas -1 means sell order as it implies the decline.

Two experiments to predict the index movement direction are presented. Experiment 1 is to use market data, which include opening price, closing price, high for the day, low for the day, trading volume in the number of shares, trading volume in RMB, change in RMB, and change in percentage. Then, we combine them with sentiment features for Experiment 2. We employ classification accuracy Acc to assess the performance, as shown by

$$
Acc = \frac{T_{++} + T_{--}}{T_{++} + T_{--} + F_{-+} + F_{+-}}, \tag{4.17}
$$

where T_{++} denotes the true value of $+1$ and the prediction value is also $+1$; T_{--} denotes the true value of -1, and the prediction value is also -1; F_{+-} denotes the true value of $+1$, whereas the prediction value is -1; F_{-+} denotes the true value of -1, whereas the prediction value is $+1$.

Five-fold cross-validation approach is adopted to train SVM model. Eventually, the proper parameters and the kernel functions to achieve the best performance were identified, yielding Figs. 4.1 and 4.2,

Table 4.2 documents the processes of parameter selection. Panel A of Table 4.2 shows prediction results. For Experiment 1, the accuracy was 79.96% using the RBF kernel function $C = 256$, $\gamma = 0.9942$; for Experiment 2, the accuracy was 97.73%, using RBF kernel function $C = 181.0193$, $\gamma = 0.005524$.

However, the two kinds of methods cannot be applied in forecasting stock market movement direction for the reason that they lead to look-ahead bias, which is created by the use of information or data that would not have been known or available during

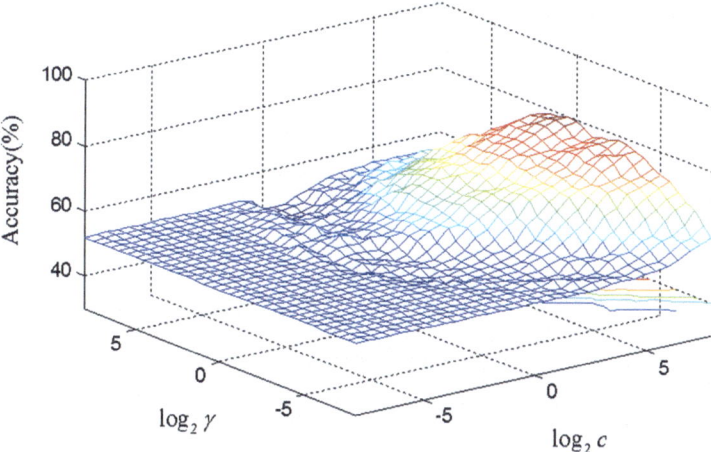

Fig. 4.1 Parameter selection process for Experiment 1

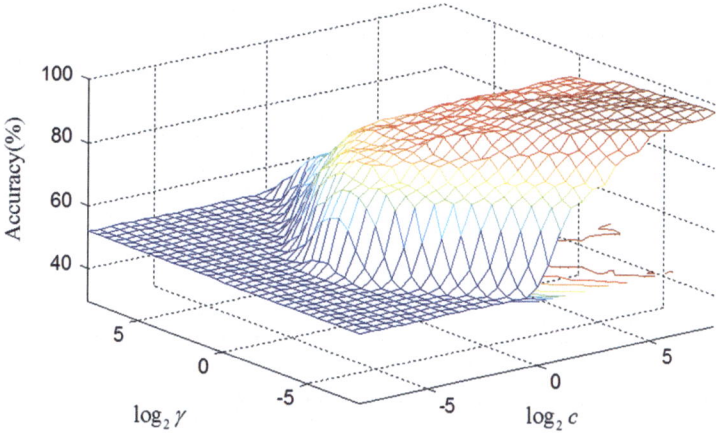

Fig. 4.2 Parameter selection process for Experiment 2

the period being analyzed. For example, data from January to May were modeled using five-fold cross-validation approach. Using data from February to May as a training set and data in January as the testing set would be impossible because, in January, there is no knowledge of what will happen from February to May. On the other hand, this does not mean that the method is useless. It is an important procedure to select the proper kernel functions and parameters as well as address the overfitting problem. In other words, the purpose of the procedure is not to forecast but select the proper kernel functions and parameters.

A realistic rolling window was used to overcome the challenge. Accordingly, a single best window for both experiments was identified. The principle of choosing the rolling windows is that n previous days are used to forecast the next day's

Table 4.2 Prediction results

Panel A: Prediction accuracy of SVM with five-fold cross validation			
	Accuracy	C	γ
Experiment 1	0.7996	256	0.9942
Experiment 2	0.9773	181.0193	0.0055

Panel B: Prediction accuracy of SVM with rolling windows				
	Accuracy	C	γ	Rolling window
Experiment 1	0.7133	256	0.9942	68
Experiment 2	0.8993	181.0193	0.0055	76

Panel C: Prediction accuracy of LR with five-fold cross validation			
	Accuracy	Max	Optimization
Experiment 1	0.7096	600	Gradient descent
Experiment 2	0.8659	1000	Stochastic gradient descent

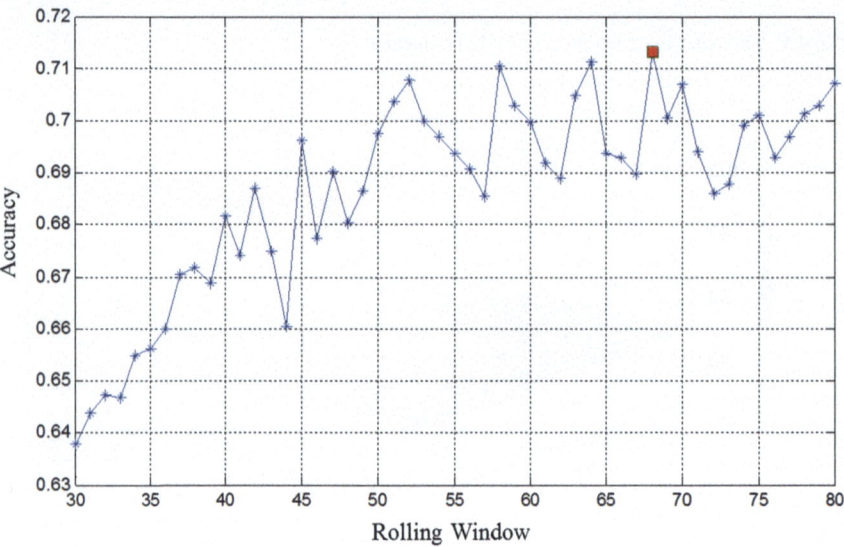

Fig. 4.3 Rolling window selection for Experiment 1

movement direction, repeating the procedure and changing the value of n until the SVM model achieves the highest accuracy with the parameters and the kernel function selected. Figures 4.3 and 4.4 display the rolling window choosing processes. For Experiment 1, the optimal rolling window is 68 and the highest accuracy is 71.33%; for Experiment 2, the optimal rolling window is 76 and the highest accuracy is 89.93%. It is clear from each figure that the accuracy is relatively stable at around the optimal rolling window. It remains lower than the highest accuracy after 80 days in Fig. 4.3 or 90 days in Fig. 4.4, which are not shown in the figures due to scale.

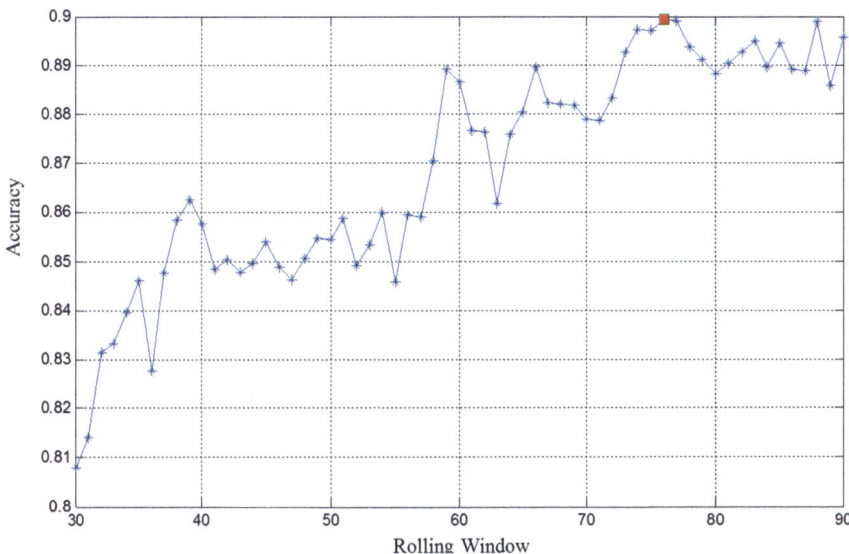

Fig. 4.4 Rolling window selection for Experiment 2

Panel B of Table 4.2 sheds light on the prediction accuracy of SVM with rolling windows. Adding sentiment features to the baseline model helps boost the prediction performance significantly. The reasons why the empirical result of forecasting the market index movement direction can be as high as 89.93% probably include that investor sentiment plays a very important role in the stock market. Furthermore, sentiment contains valuable knowledge about the asset values and can be considered as one of the leading indicators of the stock market.

In addition, a logistic regression (LR) was used to reexamine conclusions. LR is a very important method in prediction, and it is good at modeling the probability of a response based on a set of predictor variables. In order to compare with SVM, five-fold cross-validation is also applied to forecast the movement direction of the SSE 50 Index. For Experiment 1, the accuracy is 70.96% and gradient descent (GD) with the maximum number of iterations set to 600 is implemented to converge the result; for Experiment 2, the accuracy is 86.59% and stochastic gradient descent (SGD) with the maximum number of iterations set to 1000 is implemented to converge the result. Panel C of Table 4.2 confirms that investor sentiment is vital for the stock prices and illustrates that the accuracy of LR with five-fold cross-validation is acceptable, but it is not only less than SVM with five-fold cross-validation but also less than SVM with a rolling window approach, suggesting that our method is realistic and efficient.

4.4.4 Investment Performance

This section tries to discover if the prediction results are of benefit to the investment. Some measures are employed to evaluate and compare the performance of the methods. Accumulated income (AI) is computed based on the stock points. For example, if we buy a stock at the price of 100 and sell it at 150, then we earn 50 stock points and AI is 50 stock points; after that, we short the equity at 150 and liquidate the position at 120; then, we make 30 stock points, and AI becomes 80 stock points. Max drawdown (MDD) is the maximum decline of a series from a peak to a trough over a specified time period. MDD at time T is expressed as

$$\text{MDD} = \sup_{t\in[0,T]} \left[\sup_{s\in[0,t]} X(s) - X(t) \right], \qquad (4.18)$$

where $X(t)$ is a random process on $[0, T]$. MDD time illustrates when MDD occurs. The expected maximum drawdown (EMD) is an estimate of the maximum loss average, based on a geometric Brownian motion assumption. MDD and EMD are regarded as indicators of downside risk. Sharpe ratio (SR) is a way to gauge the performance of an investment by calculating the adjusted-risk return defined as

$$\text{SR} = \frac{r_a - r_f}{\sigma_a}, \qquad (4.19)$$

where r_a is the mean of the asset returns, σ_a is the standard deviation of the asset returns, and r_f denotes the risk-free rate and set to be 0 in this paper.

Label 1 is associated with a buy order, while -1 is associated with a sell order. Prediction results indicate buy or sell, and then, the process is to find if it is beneficial to support investment decisions and reduce financial risk. Short selling mechanism is allowed, and there are no market frictions. The prediction results of Experiment 1 and Experiment 2 are utilized to compute AI and MDD, respectively. Figures 4.5 and 4.6 demonstrate AI compared to the trend of the closing price of the SSE 50 Index and highlight the max drawdown district of AI simultaneously. It can be seen from the line graphs and Table 4.3 that AI of Experiment 2 (916.6264 stock points) is more than two times of Experiment 1 (404.8598 stock points). Moreover, although both the methods fail to detect the dramatic decline at first, Experiment 2 predicts the trend afterward and is able to uncover the following rise. The sharp decrease is known as the Chinese stock market crash in 2015. Besides, MDD of Experiment 2 is 0.3770, whereas MDD of Experiment 1 is 0.4073. Similarly, EMD of the next thirty days for Experiment 2 (0.1882) is also lower than that for Experiment 1 (0.2546). This implies that sentiment features help to reduce risks for investors and institutions. In addition, SR significantly went up by adding sentiment variables, which indicates that the results of Experiment 2 can help investors make higher profits with the same risk.

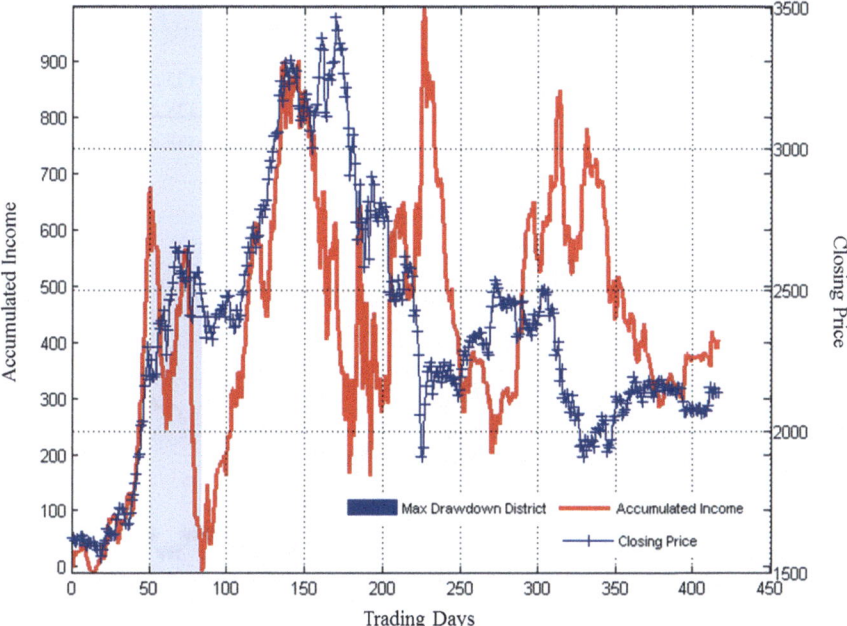

Fig. 4.5 Accumulated income from Experiment 1

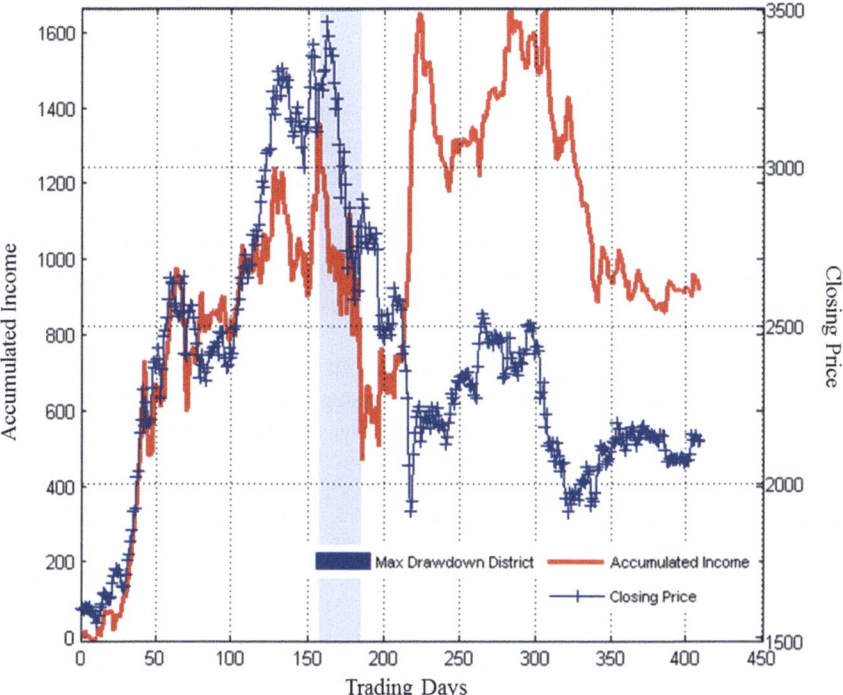

Fig. 4.6 Accumulated income from Experiment 2

Table 4.3 Investment performance

	AI	SR	MDD	MDD	EMD
Experiment 1	404.86	0.3263	0.4073	50–85 (35 days)	0.2546
Experiment 2	916.63	0.8263	0.3770	157–185 (28 days)	0.1882
Experiment 3 (strategy)	1300.46	1.2248	0.3034	306–384 (78 days)	0.1572

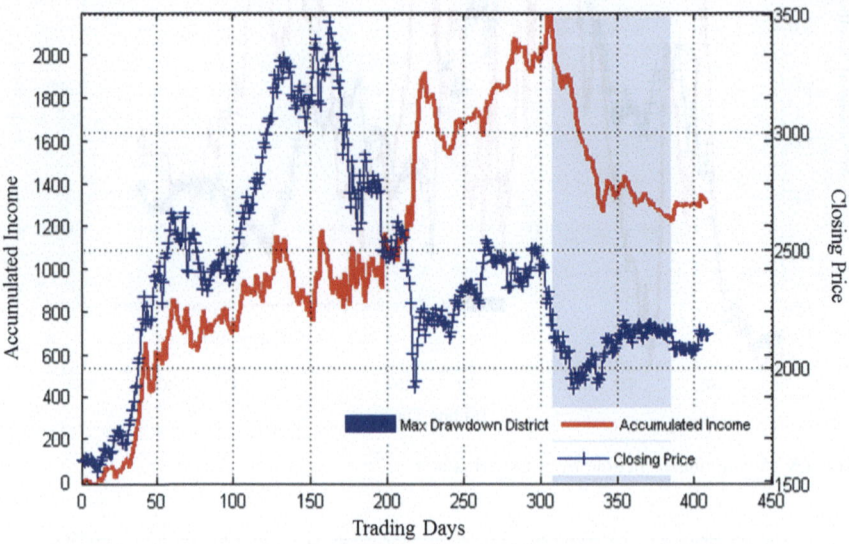

Fig. 4.7 Stop loss order strategy for Experiment 2

Finally, better performance is sought based on the prediction results of Experiment 2. Hence, a stop loss order strategy is applied to limit potential losses. Stop order was set at 95 stock points, which means that stopping to trade if 95 stock points had already been lost in a trading day. The strategy accomplishes a much better performance, and all the measures that are displayed in the third row of Table 4.3 improve significantly. From Figs. 4.6 and 4.7, a stop loss order can put an end to a losing period, but it cannot turn it into a win. However, the reduced loss also means an increase in a final accumulated income.

As a result, this approach can be of great benefit to investors if combined with a proper strategy, for example, a stop loss order strategy. In other words, the method is useful for decision making processes that are pervasive phenomena of nature.

4.5   Conclusion

Text mining and sentiment analysis have been successfully applied to stock market analysis, capable of recommending buy/sell actions while monitoring social media data in real time. Such data tend to be complex, with nonlinear relationships.

Recommender systems can include SVM models to fit such data. This is germane to epidemiology where many diseases appear, some of which can turn into pandemics. The data are complex, as thankfully most such diseases do not turn into pandemics. When they do, however, we have seen with COVID-19 that the impact can be severe. Just as social media can be monitored to support stock market decisions as demonstrated in this chapter, so can epidemiology. Web crawlers can gather data in real time, feeding into data mining models to identify optimal policies.

References

1. Liu, B., & Zhang, L. (2012). A survey of opinion mining and sentiment analysis. In: Aggarwal, C.C., Zhai, C. (eds) *Mining Text Data.* (springer, Heidelberg, pp. 415-463).
2. Kelly, F. C. (2003). *Why you win or lose: The psychology of speculation.* Courier Corporation.
3. Huang, W., Nakamori, Y., & Wang, S.-Y. (2005). Forecasting stock market movement direction with support vector machine. *Computers and Operations Research, 32*(10), 2513–2522.
4. Yu, L., Chen, H., Wang, S., & Lai, K. K. (2009). Evolving least squares support vector machines for stock market trend mining. *IEEE Transactions on Evolutionary Computation, 13*(1), 87–102.
5. Cortes, C., & Vapnik, V. (1995). Support-vector networks. *Machine Learning, 20*, 273–297.

Chapter 5
Macroeconomic Impact

Abstract Pandemics create strain on economies, due to the need to provide medical resources as well as the need to control the population to halt disease spread. COVID-19 created an extremely severe strain on economies throughout the world due to its high degree of contagion and governmental response advocated by the World Health Organization stressing lockdowns. The governmental financial response has been extreme. This chapter reviews macroeconomic policy options to combat pandemics.

COVID-19 quickly spread across global supply chains, creating a need for governmental moves to strict social distancing, which resulted in rapid declines in demands [1]. But the pandemic caught the world off-guard, creating an unprecedented shock. To counteract the resulting business shutdowns and unemployment, governments have adopted different forms of bailouts. McKinsey reported vast parts and labor shortages, leading to supply chain disruptions. The International Monetary Fund (IMF) noted that the economic crisis was in large part due to these containment measures, creating a different role for economic policy [2]. Oxford Economics [3] noted the unprecedented scale and speed of the economic impact on the Asia-Pacific region. This in part was due to the Asia-focused global supply chain, where the lockdowns in the first quarter of 2020 likely provided the sharpest contraction in world economic output in history, with the second quarter of 2020 likely to be worse as countries throughout the world adopted ambitious policy responses. However, Oxford Economics also noted that recovery appeared underway in China early in the second quarter of 2020.

The IMF expects the worst recession since the 1930s, with partial recovery in 2021. Their worst-case scenario sees a long effort to control the pandemic, hitting emerging economies the most. They expect firm closures and extended unemployment, despite the existence of a stronger global financial security network. That view sees:

Phase 1:   Containment and stabilization
Phase 2:   Recovery

D. D. Wu, D. L. Olson, *Pandemic Risk Management in Operations and Finance*,
Computational Risk Management, https://doi.org/10.1007/978-3-030-52197-4_5

Table 5.1 COVID-19 economic impact

	IMF (%) [2]	Oxford (%) [3]
Drop in global GDP-2020	3.0	2.8
Increase in 2021	5.8	6.0

Phase 1 was expected to include quarantines, lockdowns, and social distancing to control the expected surge of hospital cases. This phase was not expected to end until a vaccine was developed. Governments have adopted broad-based stimulus and liquidity support, but massive unemployment was expected to linger. The IMF and Oxford [3] provided similar projections of the economic impact of COVID-19 (see Table 5.1):

These projections were contingent on the pandemic fading in the second half of 2020. Global financial markets were expected to tighten and spending patterns were expected to shift, with a negative impact on confidence in the economy along with volatile commodity prices. Governments would face increased health care expenditure, with the need to cushion the impact on people, firms, and the financial system. Risks to fiscal operations included:

- More severe economic fallout from repeated outbreaks and spreading of the pandemic throughout the world
- Large swings in commodity prices (oil has already plummeted in price due to a price war, followed by the disappearance of demand from lockdowns)
- Prolonged stress in global financial markets
- Social unrest
- Extreme weather is difficult to cope with

5.1   Policy Options

Governments can apply two broad forms of policy controls to promote economic and financial stability: monetary and fiscal. Monetary policy is implemented through control of the money supply and the central bank interest level. In times of crisis, the central bank can increase the quantity of money to provide liquidity to financial markets in order to provide funding access to business. A feature of monetary policy across the world is that the interest rates have been dropped close to zero, limiting the ability of central banks to apply much monetary policies in that manner. The US Federal Reserve Bank lowered the short-term rate to zero on 15 March 2020. Another measure of control is available through quantitative easing, involving large-scale asset purchases of securities by central banks. Following the 2008 mortgage lending crisis, the US Federal Reserve increased securities holding by $3.7 trillion [4]. On 23 March 2020, the US Federal Reserve announced a policy to increase purchases of Treasury securities and mortgage-backed securities at the rate of up to $125 billion daily, which would project it to exceed the peak of $4.5 trillion after the post financial crisis. However, the downside to quantitative easing is that it benefits the wealthy holders of securities, thus increasing income disparity [5].

Other actions to provide liquidity include reduction of reserve requirements, allowing banks to loan more money. On 15 March 2020, the Federal Reserve lowered reserve requirements to zero, for the first time ever. The downside of this action is that reserve requirements were a key component of financial system risk management. Another device available to the Federal Reserve is lending cash through repurchase agreements (repos) with large government security dealers. Following the financial crisis of 2008, the large balance sheet generated by the Federal Reserve meant that such lending was no longer needed. But on September 2019, this mechanism was revived, and on 12 March 2020, the Federal Reserve announced that it would offer a three-month repo of $500 billion and a one-month repo of $500 billion on a weekly basis through that month in addition to shorter-term repos that it had already been offering. The Federal Reserve also encouraged insured deposit institutions to borrow from its discount window to meet liquidity needs, playing the role of lender of last resort. Finally, on 17 March 2020, the Federal Reserve revived purchase of commercial paper to provide short-term funding to business.

Fiscal policy involves providing funding directly to the economy, in the form of development of infrastructure (supporting construction) or directly to individuals. Congress appropriated $8.3 billion in emergency funding on 5 March 2020 to support the fight against COVID-19, signed by President Trump on 6 March 2020. President Trump also signed the Families First Coronavirus Response Act on 18 March 2020 to provide paid sick leave and free coronavirus testing, expansion of food assistance and unemployment benefits, and requirement for employers to provide additional protections for healthcare workers. Additionally, low-interest loans were offered to small businesses and tax payment penalties deferred for businesses affected by COVID-19. Disaster funding was provided to states and local governments through the declaration of a state of emergency. The Defense Production Act was invoked, giving the President authority to require some US businesses to increase the production of medical equipment and supplies.

The Coronavirus Aid, Relief, and Economic Security Act provided $1200 tax rebates to individuals with additional $500 per qualifying child to those with incomes below $75,000 ($150,000 if married filing jointly). It also provided funding for forgivable bridge loans to small businesses, as well as emergency loans to distressed business such as air carriers. Unemployment insurance benefits were increased with expanded eligibility. Federal student loan payments were temporarily suspended. Funding was provided for the prevention, diagnosis, and treatment of COVID-19.

The IMF staff came up with a suggestion for governments to cope with the pandemic, contingent upon their fiscal ability as well as the adequacy of their social support systems;

For firms, solvency issues could be dealt with through equity injection grants. Liquidity issues could involve tax relief, wage subsidies, and direct loans to smaller firms if ample fiscal room was available. Should fiscal capabilities be limited, umbrella guaranteed loans by public banks could be applied.

For households, governments with low coverage and adequacy of their social system could apply one-time universal transfers, in-kind provision of goods and services (especially health), wage subsidies, and tax deferrals. If social coverage was higher, social safety net systems could be scaled up, with relaxed eligibility criteria. If fiscal opportunities were more limited, social safety nets could be strengthened with sector- or place-based transfers to hard-hit areas and industries, as well as the direct provision of basic needs. If the social system had higher development, coverage and benefit levels of existing programs could be expanded.

5.2   Global Response

Asian countries have faced the same issues but from slightly different situations. Japan has had very low interest rates for some time and has little if any room to apply the mechanism of lower interest rates. The Bank of Japan instead injected $4.6 billion into Japanese banks to enable short-term loans and about $9 billion into exchange-traded funds to support Japanese businesses [6]. Wage subsidies were pledged for parents forced to take time off due to school closures. The 2020 Summer Olympics scheduled to be held in Tokyo were postponed for a year.

In China, the impact of countering COVID-19 has made it likely that their economic growth as measured by GDP would be negative for the first quarter of 2020 and lower expected growth to less than 5% for 2020 [7]. If the outbreak continues or becomes more serious, this could be worse. The Chinese central bank injected $57 billion into their banking system while capping bank interest rates on loans for major firms. Banks had been given deadlines to curb shadow loans, but this deadline was extended. On 13 March 2020, The People's Bank of China announced $78.8 billion in funding by reducing bank reserve requirements.

European countries have not had the synchronized policy response that they developed during the 2008–2009 financial crisis. A variety of policies have been applied, to include quarantines and business closures, travel and border restrictions, tax holidays for businesses, subsidies for workers, and loan guarantees. A corona bond has been proposed as a joint European debt instrument, but this has been opposed by Germany, the Netherlands, and others. The Bank of England adopted a package of four elements, including cutting the interest rate, introduction of a Term Funding Scheme for small and medium-sized enterprises, lowering bank capital buffers to zero percent, and freezing of bank dividend payments. Fiscal spending was increased nearly $3.5 billion to include sick leave funding. Emergency funding was provided to the National Health Service.

5.3 Summary

COVID-19 is expected to have a major impact in setting back global economic development. Obviously, the longer lockdowns are imposed, the greater the economic impact. There is evidence of economic recovery in China. If some areas of the global economy begin to recover, there might be less reticence to wait before opening up economies on the part of other regions or countries. The choice is complete safety and starvation or coping with what nature throws at us and move on.

References

1. McKinsey & Company. (2020, March 25). *COVID-19: Briefing note—Global health and crisis response*. McKinsey & Company.
2. International Monetary Fund. (2020, April). *World economic outlook: Chapter 1—The great lockdown*. International Monetary Fund.
3. Oxford Economics. (2020, April). *The economic impact of COVID-19 on Asia Pacific*. Oxford Economics.
4. Congressional Research Service. (2020, March 26). *Global economic effects of COVID-19 R46270*. Congressional Research Service. https://crsreports.congress.gov.
5. Paul, J.-M. (2019). *The economics of discontent*. Solvau Brussels School of Economics and Management (E-book).
6. Harding, R., & Lockett, H. (2020, March 2). BoJ spurs Asia markets rebound with vow to fight coronavirus. *Financial Times*.
7. Sutter, K. M., & Sutherland, M. D. (2020). *U.S.-China economic considerations*. CRS In Focus IF 11434.

Chapter 6
Supply Chain Impact

Abstract Network analysis was applied using Citespace software applied to downloaded data of Web-of-Science Publications. Search terms "SARS & Risk", "MERS & Risk," and "Ebola & Risk" were used. For each experiment, the network analysis used both abstract and article clustering. Tools such as risk, clinical, and healthcare are common hot spot words that were employed. Research topics focused on health care, disease, influenza, and infection. Research on economy and epidemics is not in the core of the network analysis results, identifying a need for research effort.

6.1 Pandemic Disruption

Economic disruption risk from many sources (natural and man-made) has occurred throughout history [1]. The ability to cope with disruption events through recovery policies is crucial. This includes proactive design and planning of robust and resilient supply chains with recovery policies [2]. Prediction of uncertain events impacting supply chains and identification of means to restore them are critical for coping with disruption propagation. Robust supply chains can absorb disturbances and continue to function. Resilient supply chains develop the ability to sustain operations and restore functionality and performance.

Critical aspects of supply chain disruptions have been proposed: high profile disruptions; increased impact as a result of lean operations and supply chains; and an increase in sourcing over vertical integration [3]. Regardless of the type of disruption, results are typically modeled in relation to individual supply chains or organizations rather than the economy as a whole.

Revilla and Saenz [4] studied national versus global impacts of supply chain disruptions, finding that more integrated and developed supply chains take on cultural similarities even as they cross borders. While providing a framework for analysis, modeling remains at the individual supply chain level. Risk of supply chain disruptions, both actual and perceived, from both internal and external sources must be addressed, but different disruptions require different reactions by organizations

D. D. Wu, D. L. Olson, *Pandemic Risk Management in Operations and Finance*,
Computational Risk Management, https://doi.org/10.1007/978-3-030-52197-4_6

within supply chains. Firm resilience to supply chain disruption does make a difference. Ambulkar et al. [5] provided a measurement for resilience. As with other studies, the measurement focuses on individual firms and supply chains. The impact of supply chain disruptions on the overall economy within and across countries remains difficult to compare. Even with the current impact of COVID-19, confounding factors like threats of tariffs, actual changes in tariffs, and altered trade agreements make it difficult to impossible to identify direct causes of economic impact.

The SARS epidemic is the closest analogy with respect to impacting trade between China and the world. Figure 6.1 shows a quick recap of annual trade figures. Note little impact in the 2002–2003 period when SARS was active. There is a much greater impact in the 2008–2010 period due to economic causes.

But the world has become much leaner and more connected. COVID-19 has been followed by significant panic in the financial market, not all necessarily due to COVID-19. For instance, the oil market has suffered a massive price drop, in part but not entirely due to a drop in demand.

The experience in China in 2003 due to SARS demonstrated in Fig. 6.2 was a clear drop that proved to be temporary. Even that drop still included a high rate of economic growth. The economic duration appears to be in the range of 6 months, in a very rough interpretation. Many firms in China shifted from offline retail to e-business in response to the impact of business interruption and cash flow insufficiency. The Internet also became a platform for many offline transactions. We might expect a similar impact from COVID-19, although the more linked global economy might involve higher variance than that was experienced in 2003.

Reports from the Internet identify a major impact on supply chains. On 3 February, there were posts that the automotive industry has resulted in lower production for Honda, PSA Group, and Dongfeng Motors due to COVID-19. Hyundai has suspended production in South Korea due to the disruption of part supply from Asia. On 5 February, it was noted that there were significant delays in shipping due to governmental prevention and control measures. Airports, highways, railways, and ports have been affected. About 80% of world goods trade is carried by sea, and China has a majority of the world's 10 busiest container ports. This creates stress for members of supply chains, threatening small vendors who have less capital reserves. Another impact is the spread of misinformation through social media. There are increased freight costs due to rerouting, and closure of manufacturing in affected areas in Asia has a major ripple effect on the world economy.

On 6 February, it was reported that Airbus, Toyota, General Motors, and Volkswagen were all closing some Chinese production. Nintendo was worried about the supply of consoles and controllers. Apple devices from Foxconn Technology were expected to be shut down for at least a week. Airlines were reducing flights, as were freighter operators.

By 11 February, it was noted that uncertainty of virus spread had resulted in unprecedented measures in shipping and precipitous rate declines. In Shanghai and Hong Kong, only about half of dockworkers returned to work. Global Port Tracker reports that projected US container volume in February would fall nearly 13% from

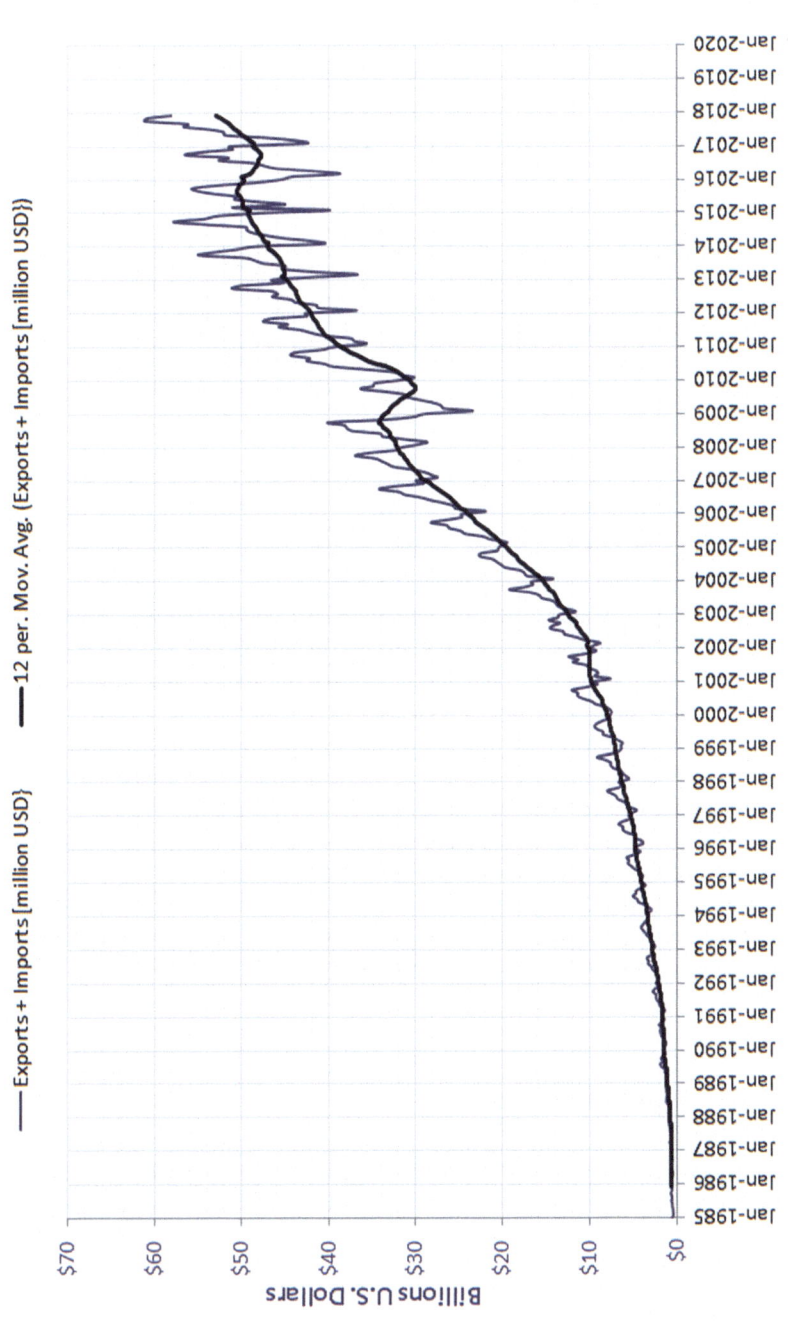

Fig. 6.1 Combined value of U.S. exports to China and imports from China, January 1985–December 2017. https://seekingalpha.com/article/4146952 based on US Census data

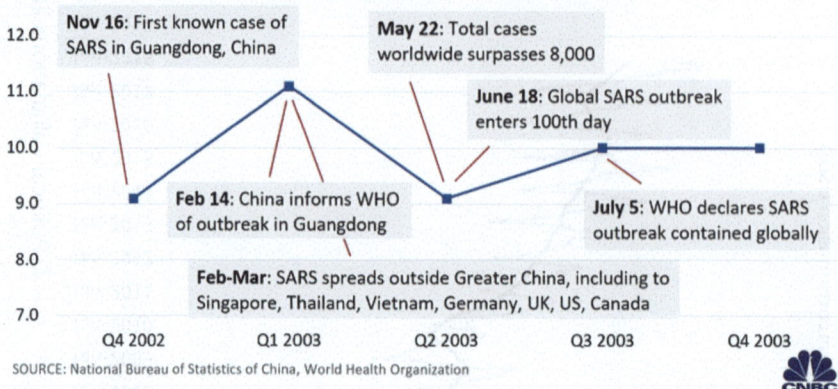

China's economic growth during SARS
Line shows the year-on-year percentage change in real growth

Nov 16: First known case of SARS in Guangdong, China

May 22: Total cases worldwide surpasses 8,000

June 18: Global SARS outbreak enters 100th day

Feb 14: China informs WHO of outbreak in Guangdong

July 5: WHO declares SARS outbreak contained globally

Feb-Mar: SARS spreads outside Greater China, including to Singapore, Thailand, Vietnam, Germany, UK, US, Canada

SOURCE: National Bureau of Statistics of China, World Health Organization

CNBC

Fig. 6.2 CNBC graph posted on https://www.cnbc.com/2020/02/11/coronavirus-4-charts

2019 and almost 10% in March. Tet typically pushes back work up to 4 weeks, and this COVID-19 has added another 3 weeks of delay.

Impact on supply chains calls for obtaining alternative sources. Moving to alternatives takes time and added cost. But that is something that a viable economic system can overcome with time. What has been most surprising is the governmental reaction in the form of lockdown of human activity as the only means of trying to halt the spread of the virus.

Disruptions of supply chains cause stress throughout the system due to correlation of risk, cyclical linkages, counterparty risk, and other systemic misalignments. Such disruptions can involve long-term economic and social consequence, with slow recovery that can significantly affect financial performance.

Mitigation of supply chain disruption has been found to be improved through better information management and risk sharing across supply chain participants [6]. The sharing of risk is determined by participant negotiating power.

6.2 Network Analysis

Network analysis is a text mining tool to identify words that have a relatively high correlation in a textual dataset. Using Citespace software, Web-of-Science publications were searched to identify the relative density of research on risk aspects of previous epidemics SARS, MERS, and Ebola.

6.2.1 SARS

SARS is a type of coronavirus. Its symptoms include fever, chills, headaches, body aches, shortness of breath, and dry cough, much as those symptoms of flu and pneumonia. It appears to have originated in Guangdong Province in mid-November 2002. Chou et al. [7] estimated 8422 cases in 32 countries that led to 916 deaths, for a mortality rate of 0.109. A distinguishing feature of SARS was a high infection rate among health care workers treating SARS patients (at least before the implementation of protective measures). Early diagnosis is the best way to stop infection of health workers. There is no specific treatment, and most patients were treated similar to those with serious atypical pneumonia. Chest X-rays and blood tests 28 days after illness onset were used to diagnose probable SARS cases.

Chou et al. [7] examined the economic impact of SARS on Taiwan's economy. They reported that nearly 30% of international flights into Taiwan were canceled during the outbreak, reducing passenger count by 122,000 in the second quarter of 2003. Hotel occupancy rates dropped 30% in March 2003, and recreational and eating establishments suffered. Additionally, people reduced spending, and Chinese export orders slowed to their lowest pace in over a year. Johanis [8] reported that the impact of SARS on the economy of Toronto was devastating to travel and tourism. They constructed a model to predict the impact on Taiwan GDP for both short-term (less than 1 year) and longer-term outbreaks, based on simulation. Their model predicted a short-term drop in GDP of 0.67% for Taiwan, 0.20% for China, and 1.56% for Hong Kong. The longer-term model resulted in a predicted additional 1.6% drop in Chinese GDP. Figure 6.3 shows the network analysis results:

It can be seen that SARS generated a great deal of academic research over the period 1998 to 2008. The rows of Fig. 6.3 show the topic focus given on the right. As expected, focus on the key topic is heaviest, but there is overlap as well. The takeaway is that recognition and control strategies are of great interest.

6.2.2 MERS

MERS appeared in September 2012 in Saudi Arabia but was confined mostly to the Arabian Peninsula. In over 1300 confirmed MERS cases in over 20 countries, there were at least 471 fatalities as of June 2015 for a mortality rate of an alarming 0.36 probability. In June 2015, over 100 cases appeared in South Korea. Within a month, over 180 cases had resulted in 36 deaths, for a mortality rate of 0.19 [9]. Published research on the citizen reaction to the government response to the South Korean outbreak indicates anger, anxiety, and cynicism [10]. Yang [11] noted low credibility of risk information and prevalent rumors in the media. In part, this appears to be influenced by general trust in the government.

Lim [9] noted that while there is still no MERS cure, development of drugs and vaccines is underway. That author also noted that Saudi Arabia has implemented

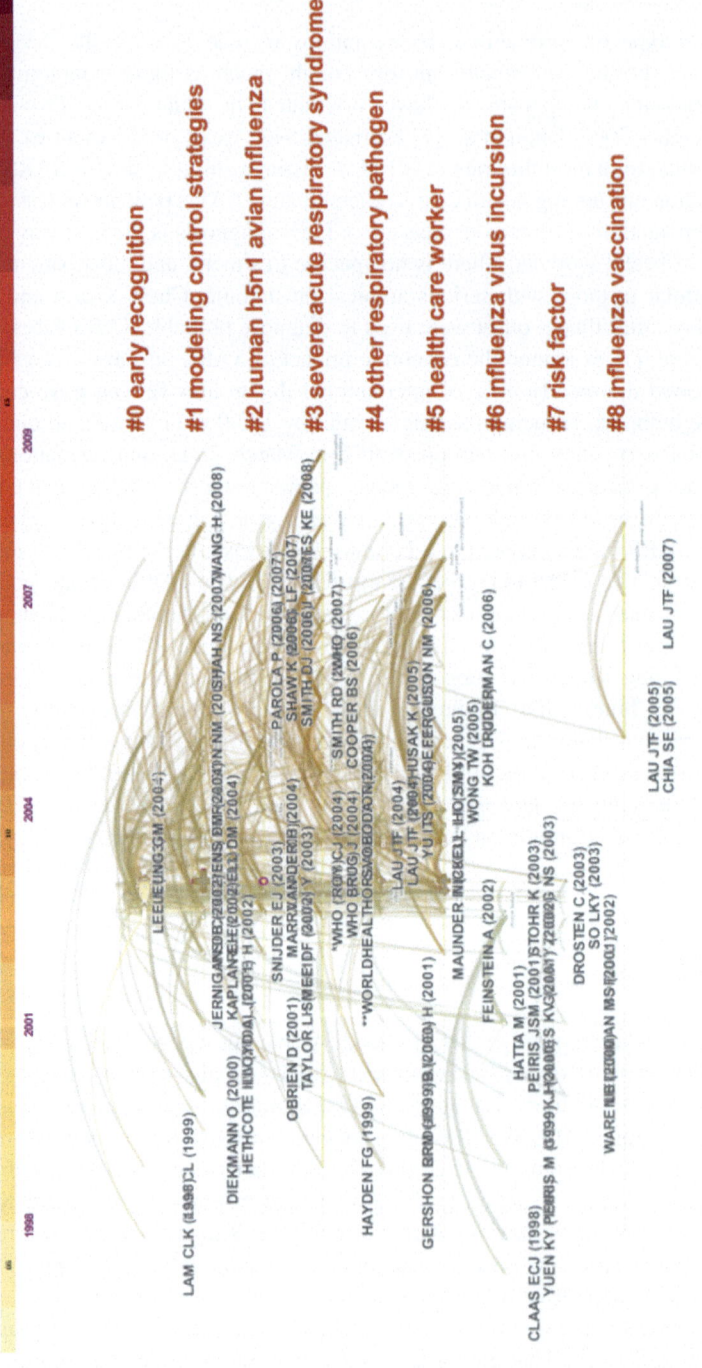

Fig. 6.3 Abstract network clustering for "SARS & Risk"

control actions to include crowd control, vigilant monitoring, and early isolation for participants in hajj, which, in 2012, was the site of the initial outbreak. Pilgrims from noted risk areas, such as Thailand and Singapore, were required to obtain influenza vaccination before leaving their home country. Figure 6.4 shows the network analysis results for MERS.

In Fig. 6.4, there are fewer topics, but continuous interest is shown. Preventive measures and risk factors are growing in interest.

6.2.3 Ebola

The Ebola virus disease epidemic in West Africa struck over the period of 2013–2016, with some small spreading to the US and Europe. As of 2018, it led to over 28,000 cases with over 11,000 deaths, an alarming mortality rate approaching 0.4 [12]. Ebola first appeared in 1976 in what was then Zaire, the longest and largest to date. Quarantines were implemented, ending the epidemic after nearly 300 died. In 1995, Ebola again appeared in Zaire at Kikwit, which was isolated by the Zaire government. This epidemic ended after 9 months after 250 died. By 2014, there had been at least 16 more Ebola outbreaks across the Congo basin and Uganda [13]. But response ability had not notably improved, with no vaccine and inability to rapidly diagnose cases. Calnan et al. [12] summarized issues created by Ebola (Table 6.1):

Figure 6.5 shows the results of the network clustering for Ebola.

Continuous interest in virus disease to identify Ebola is observed. Calnan et al. [12] identified challenges from the Ebola outbreak, to include communication difficulties, local infrastructure problems, health system response, lack of cooperation with international agencies, and security challenges. Those authors developed a risk model considering the following risk criteria:

- Gross domestic product (GDP)
- Health expenditure as a percentage of GDP
- History of war/civil unrest in the past decade
- Use of traditional healers and high-risk practices
- Unsafe animal handling
- Physician density
- Density of nurses and midwives
- Density of skilled health care workers
- Diagnostic availability
- Quarantine system and border security

This model was used to score risk in countries where Ebola appeared. The intent was to predict the impact of infectious disease outbreaks. Guinea, Liberia, and Sierra Leone were the highest risk countries identified.

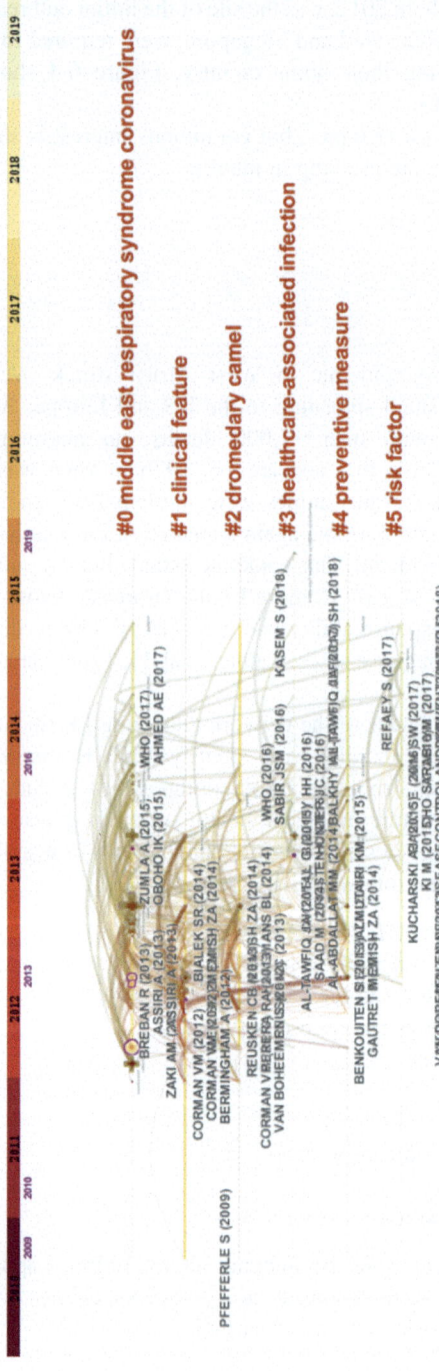

Fig. 6.4 Abstract network clustering for "MERS & Risk"

Table 6.1 Impact of Ebola

Theme	Issues
Family	Broken families
	Stigma
Relationships	Stigmatization
	Community reintegration difficulties
	Secrecy and isolation
Health	Joint pain
	Trembling
	Fever
	Insomnia
	Memory
	Vision
	Fatigue
Economics	Loss of accommodations
	Loss of work
	Restriction of economic activities
	Reduced work performance
Wellbeing	Traumatization
	Isolation
	Stress
	Unhappiness

6.2.4 COVID-19

As with SARS (and COVID-19), symptoms commonly are fever and cough frequently leading to lower respiratory tract disease with poor clinical outcomes for older patients or those with underlying health conditions. As with SAS and COVID-19, no antiviral therapies have been identified. Most secondary transmission of SARS and MERS occurred in hospital settings. Health workers in China have been hard hit, with 1716 confirmed cases and 5 deaths as of 11 February 2020 [14]. But most spread occurs due to close human contacts. COVID-10 appears more transmissible than SARS and MERS. Epidemiology uses the metric R_0 as a basic reproduction number measuring contagiousness. R_0 represents the number of secondary cases that can be expected to be generated by a single infection in a completely susceptible population, a product of transmissibility (probability of infection when a susceptible individual comes into contact with an infected individual), the rate of contact between susceptible and infective individuals, and the duration of infectiousness [15]. Related to that is the SIR model used for modeling the trajectory of an epidemic [16]. It is a Markov chain of three groups: susceptible, infected, and those leaving the system through either immunization or death. It is affected by the number of contacts per day (transmissibility times rate of contact) and by the fraction of the infected group that will recover on a given day (the inverse of the rate of infectiousness). Reuters Graphics on 8 February 2020 reported COVID-119 to have a high R_0 relative to SARS or MERS. In 1 month in Wuhan, over 37,000

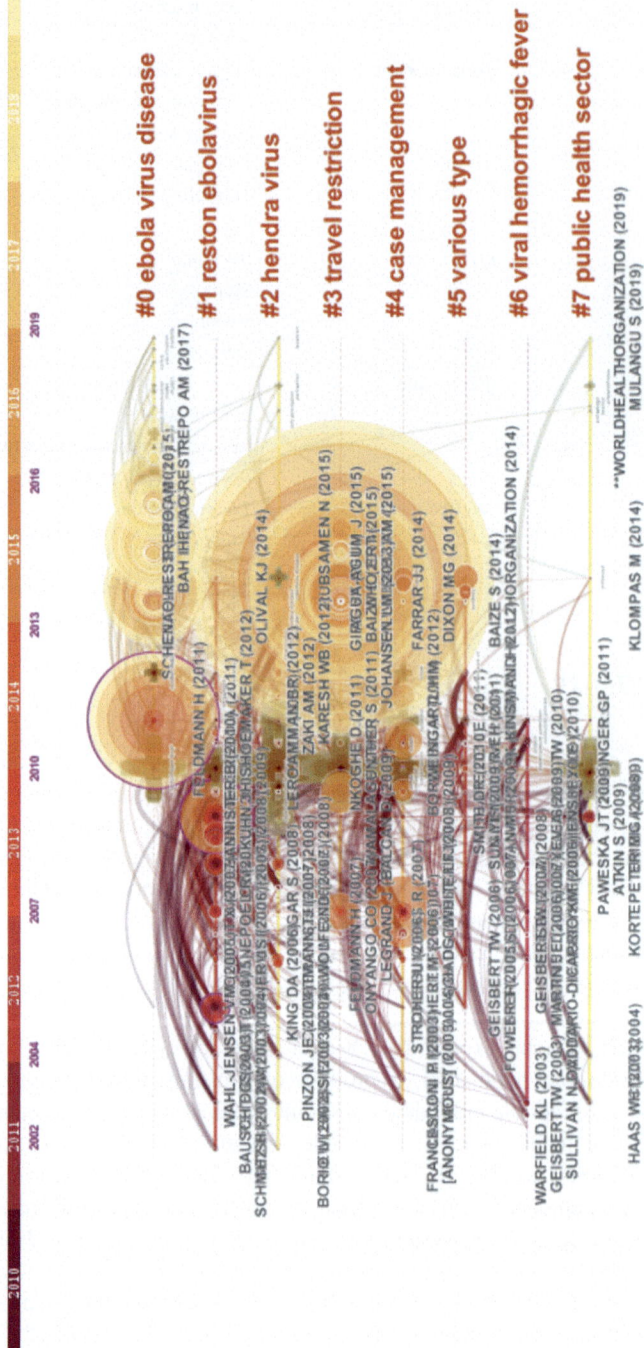

Fig. 6.5 Abstract network clustering for "Ebola & Risk"

people were confirmed to be infected with COVID-19. With SARS, about 8000 people were infected before the outbreak ended after 8 months. It took a year for 1106 people to be infected with MERS.

6.3   Conclusion

China has become a major supplier in many global supply chain activities. COVID-19 initially disrupted many important supply sources, causing businesses to modify supply chain arrangements. This was soon followed by spread to other major demand centers, which massively dampened the world economy.

This chapter compared the impact of previous pandemics. These were all different, in that they tended to have higher mortality rates, but not nearly the contagion found in COVID-19. But a review of these previous pandemics can demonstrate the availability of technology to monitor economic impact. Network clustering for SARS, MERS, and Ebola has been presented to monitor pandemic impact.

References

1. Ivanov, D., Dolgui, A., Sokolov, B., & Ivanova, M. (2017). Literature review on disruption recovery in the supply chain. *International Journal of Production Research, 55*(20), 6158–6174.
2. Chopra, S., & Sodhi, M. S. (2014). Reducing the risk of supply chain disruptions. *Sloan Management Review, 55*(3), 73–80.
3. Snyder, L. V., Atan, Z., Peng, P., Rong, Y., Schmitt, A. J., & Sinsoysal, B. (2016). OR/S models for supply chain disruptions: A review. *IIE Transactions, 48*(2), 89–109.
4. Revilla, E., & Saenz, M. J. (2014). Supply chain disruption management: Global convergence vs national specificity. *Journal of Business Research, 67*, 1123–1135.
5. Ambulkar, S., Blackhurst, J., & Grawe, S. (2015). Firm's resilience to supply chain disruptions: Scale development and empirical examination. *Journal of Operations Management, 33–34*, 111–122.
6. Wakolbinger, T., & Cruz, J. M. (2011). Supply chain disruption risk management through strategic information acquisition and sharing and risk-sharing contracts. *International Journal of Production Research, 49*(13), 4063–4084.
7. Chou, J., Kuo, N.-F., & Peng, S.-L. (2004). Potential impacts of the SARS outbreak on Taiwan's economy. *Asian Economic Papers, 3*(1), 84–99.
8. Johanis, D. (2007). How Toronto Pearson International airport applied lessons from SARS to develop a pandemic response plan. *Journal of Business Continuity and Emergency Planning, 1*(4), 356–368.
9. Lim, X. Z. (2015). MER outbreak. *Chemistry and Industry, 79*(8), 47.
10. Kang, M., Kim, J. R., & Cha, H. (2018). From concerned citizens to activitists: A case study of 2015 south Korean MERS outbreak and the role of dialogic government communication and citizens' emotions on public activism. *Journal of Public Relations Research, 30*(5), 202–229.
11. Yang, S.-U. (2018). Effect of government dialogic competency: The MERS outbreak and implications for public halth crises and political legitimacy. *Journalism and Mass Communication Quarterly, 95*(4), 1011–1032.

12. Calnan, M., Gadsby, E. W., Konde, M. K., Diallo, A., & Rossman, J. S. (2018). The response to and impact of the Ebola epidemic: Towards an agenda for interdisciplinary research. *International Journal of Health Policy Management, 7*(5), 402–411.
13. Garrett, L. (2015). Ebola's lessons: How the WHO mishandled the crisis. *Foreign Affairs, 94* (5), 80–107.
14. Wu, Z., & McGoogan, J. M. (2020). Summary of a report of 72314 cases from the Chinese Center for Disease Control and Prevention. *JAMA, 323*(13), 1239–1242.
15. Jones, J. H. (2007). *Notes on R_0*. Department of Anthropological Sciences, Stanford University.
16. Smith, D., & Moore, L. (2004). The SIR model for spread of disease – The differential equation model. *JOMA*.

Chapter 7
Debt Risk Analysis Using Two-Tier Networks

Abstract COVID-19 has dealt a major blow to the global economy. It would help the efforts to cope with this strain by having studies of how risk affects operations. This chapter deals with risk in the financial arena, which has been heavily hit by COVID-19. But the analysis can aid in other arenas as well, to include health-care planning and management. This study found that expansion of regional guarantee circle networks need to be controlled, as external guarantees are important to control risk contagion. Identification of key nodes in risk-contagion networks need to consider exposure and external relevance. The government should concentrate on group investment and financing platforms. And supervision of disorderly external guarantees of small- and medium-sized issuers is needed.

Nonfinancial corporate debt is one of the important sources of systematic risk in the real economy. Assessing a measure of systematic risk in corporation debt is currently a key challenge. A two-tier risk-contagion network model with four dimensions is proposed: concept definition, data structure, risk-contagion network construction, and risk measurement indicators construction. The Jiangsu bond issuer is the source of data in this study. There are strong correlations between the debts of nonfinancial corporations in China, creating it a potential source of systematic risk. This study finds that external risk exposure and the degree of network node connection are two key indicators in identifying enterprises with key risk-contagion potential.

Forestalling and defusing major risks to maintain bottom-line performance is a focus of Chinese government regulatory agencies. China's macro leverage ratio has been rising rapidly. Although a steady state was reached in 2018, as of December 2018, China's macro leverage was still above 250% [1]. Accurately measuring China's current macro leverage ratio and to attain risk prevention and resolution has urgent significance.

This chapter draws from Cao, Wu & Li (2020), Debt risk analysis of nonfinancial corporates using two-tier networks, *Industrial Management & Data Systems*, to be published, with permission.

Nonfinancial corporate debt consists primarily of bank credit and credit bonds. In recent years, the Chinese bond market has developed rapidly, and the balance of credit bonds has grown from 1.2 trillion a decade ago to about 21 trillion in the beginning of 2019. While the size of the Chinese bond market is expanding, the number and amount of bond defaults are also growing rapidly. In 2018 alone, the number and amount of defaulted bonds have exceeded twice that of 2017. Compared with traditional bank credit, bond issuers need to comply with certain information disclosure regulations, which makes the market risk of credit bonds have a strong correlation, especially credit risk arising from default events [2]. The threat of systematic risk to the financial system lies in its strong contagiousness. This threatens the Chinese economy. From this perspective, the risk of the credit bond market can spread in the financial system through mutual/joint guarantee between issuers and the information transfer mechanism of the bond market. Since issuers of credit bonds are industrial enterprises, the financial risks in this market will directly impact economic activities. Therefore, research on prevention and control of nonfinancial corporate debt risks will help prevent the risk of the debt in the economy, and thus help maintain the stability and security of the financial market.

The issuers of credit bonds form a huge network of companies through equity, debt, transaction, and guarantee relationships. From the perspective of risk-contagion mechanisms, the guarantee relationship between enterprises is an extremely important path for risk contagion. At present, the external guarantee behavior of China's bond issuers has two characteristics:

1. The average external guarantee ratio of credit bond issuers is at a high level. Higher external guarantee ratios expose companies to greater risk and weaken their ability to withstand sudden credit events.
2. Bond issuers have formed a guarantee network with a large number of external companies through a mutual guarantee or joint guarantee. Mutual guarantee or joint guarantee means that in the process of issuing bonds, each issuer adds mutual guarantees to each other's bonds to increase their credit ranking.

When a crisis occurs, in order to minimize potential losses, it is necessary to quickly and accurately identify the source of risk, the path of risk contagion, and key risk-contagion nodes within the system. Previously, the academic community mainly used the interbank market as the object of systematic risk research. This was because banks dominate the financial system in China, and the banking system has a wide micro-transaction structure that is the basic path of risk contagion. Local crises can easily be transmitted and amplified through this system and become systematic risks. However, research on risk-contagion models based on the inter-connection network of the guarantee circle in credit bond markets is not sufficient. The framework proposed in this chapter has strong theoretical significance.

7.1 Two-Tier Counterparty Risk-Contagion Network Model

Complex networks are used to analyze the risk associated with debt in nonfinancial corporation.

7.1.1 Definition of Two-Tier Counterparty Risk-Contagion Networks

In a common complex network, nodes and their connected edges are in the same layer, a single-layer complex network. In social network research, the relationship between people may have different attributes or categories. Between social-economic organizations, when an organization goes bankrupt or defaults, the organization's risks will spread through different levels of infection, such as debt and debt relations, equity guarantee relationships, information spillover relationships, and so forth. A network of two-level structure was constructed to portray the risk-contagion mechanism between economic organizations.

Diversified networks are a special type of multilayer network. The number of nodes in each layer is the same, and there is only one type of connection between layers. That is, a given node is only connected to its corresponding node in other network layers.

G is a two-layer complex network. The two layers of the G are G_h and G_m, respectively.

V is a set of all nodes in the graph, assuming the total number of nodes is N.

B is a set of all edges in graph G, where H is the set of all edges in the G_h layer, and M is the set of all edges in G_m layer. For the nodes i and j in the graph G, the edge formed by i pointing to j in the G_h layer is denoted as h_{ij}, and in the same way, the edge is denoted m_{ij} in the G_m layer.

In actual network modeling, since the edges between different nodes may have different weights, w^y_{ij} is the weight of the node i pointing to the edge of node j, where the upper corner y is the layer, $y = \{h, m\}$.

7.1.2 Division of Two-Tier Risk-Contagion Networks

In the construction of the first layer of complex networks, the guarantee relationship and the equity relationship are treated as edges. Because of the directional guarantees for the company and the holding of shares (such as i to j guarantee, or i holds shares of j), the first-tier counterparty network is directional.

Variables in this complex network system are defined as follows:

V is the set of all bond issuers, which is the set of nodes in the network, and the total
number is N;

The guarantee relationship network matrix is $L(l_{ij})$, where l_{ij} represents the guarantee
behavior of node i to node j, which is directional;

The equity relationship network matrix is $F(f_{ij})$, where the f_{ij} equal to 1 represents
i and j belong to an enterprise group;

H is the set of edges in first layer network,

$$H = \sum_{i,j \in V} h_{ij} \tag{7.1}$$

$$h_{ij} = l_{ij} + f_{ij} \tag{7.2}$$

$$H = L + F \tag{7.3}$$

M is the set of edges in second layer network,

$$M = \sum_{i,j \in V} m_{ij} \tag{7.4}$$

7.1.3 Measurement of an Organization's External Risk Exposure (ERE)

When a credit risk event occurs in a node in the network, the risk transmission from
the node to other nodes can be divided into three components:

1. The organization defaults and cannot repay the debt, so the creditor faces the loss
   of net assets; the organization guarantees this default organization will face
   responsibility for its debt repayment, resulting in liquidity output and a portion
   of net asset losses.
2. The default organization's external guarantee will invalidate, which makes the
   potential solvency of the guarantee organization decline, and may lead to trig-
   gering an early resale clause due to the failure of the relevant guarantee treaty,
   resulting in a large-scale liquidity shock.
3. When an organization falls into bankruptcy, the value of shares held by external
   organizations is lost to zero and face the risk of compensating part of the debt.

Therefore, when a credit risk event such as debt default occurs at a certain node,
its potential external risk exposure (ERE) can be expressed as follows:

$$RiskExpo_i = (G_{iO} + G_{iI}) + (D_i - A_{iL}) + (E_i * P_{iO}) \tag{7.5}$$

RiskExpo_i is the potential external exposure of the organization when it defaults, G_{iO} is the total external guarantee of the organization, G_{iI} is the external guarantee for the organization, D_i is the total liabilities of the organization, A_{iL} is the total current assets of the organization, E_i is the owner's equity, and P_{iO} is other external organization's shareholding ratio.

7.2   Risk-Contagion Channel: Node Degree

In a complex network, the number of connected edges of a node is defined as the degree of the node, and the degree k_i of the node i is the sum of the edges connected to the node i. In the undirected complex network, the attributes of each side are the same, and in a directional complex network structure, the in-degree and out-degree are the two parts of the node degree. The in-degree of node i represents the number of edges of other nodes in the network pointing to node i, and the out-degree of node i refers to the sum of the sides of node i pointing to other nodes. The connection degree of its nodes is expressed as:

$$k_i = k_i^1 + k_i^2 \tag{7.6}$$

For the two-layer network used here, the node degree is defined as follows, $k_{i(h)}$ is the degree of node i on the first layer network, and has:

$$k_{i(h)} = \sum_{j \in V} 1\{L_{ij} > 0\} + \sum_{j \in V} 1\{F_{ij} = 1\} \tag{7.7}$$

$k_{i(h)}$ is the degree of node i on the first layer network, and $k_{im)}$ is the degree of k on the second layer network, so there are:

$$k_{i(h)} = \sum_{j \in V} 1\{L_{ij} > 0\} + \sum_{j \in V} 1\{F_{ij} = 1\}; k_{i(m)} = \sum_{j \in V} 1\{M_{ij} > 0\} \tag{7.8}$$

7.2.1   Distribution of Risk-Contagion Channel: Degree Distribution

To describe the differences in the topological properties of each type of networks, the concept of degree distribution can be used. The average degree is defined as the expectation of all node degrees. $P(k)$ is commonly used to represent the distribution function of the degree of a node, that is, the ratio of the node with degree k to the number of all nodes, that is, the probability that any node in the network is exactly k.

In this two-tier risk-contagion network model, node degrees in the network represents the number of risk-contagion channels connected to other organization in the network.

7.2.2 Risk-Contagion Path: Average Shortest Path

The path length refers to the number of connected edges in the path, and the average shortest path length is the expectation of the minimum number of edges between any two points in the graph. In a network with N nodes, defined d_{ij} as the shortest path between node i and node j, the following equation represents the overall average shortest path length of the network:

$$L = \frac{1}{\frac{1}{2}N(N+1)}\sum_{i \geq j} d_{ij} \tag{7.9}$$

7.2.3 Aggregation of Risk-Contagion Network: Clustering Coefficient

The clustering coefficients can be divided into two types. The first is the global clustering coefficient proposed by Watts [3]. This index reflects the probability that any connected node of j is also connected to i when i and j are connected nodes. The second is the local clustering coefficient, which is a kind of transitivity calculation. The number of connections of the node i in the network is k_i. Calculating the maximum number of connected edges $k_i(k_i - 1)$, between the k_i nodes connected to i, and then obtain the number of connected edges between the k_i nodes from the actual network as $L_{i\,i}$, then the clustering coefficient of the node i is:

$$C_i = \frac{2L_i}{(k_i(k_i - 1))} \tag{7.10}$$

When the total number of nodes in the network is N, the global clustering coefficient is:

$$C = \frac{1}{N}\sum_i C_i \tag{7.11}$$

The construction of a two-tier counterparty risk-contagion network model is completed from four dimensions: concept definition, data structure, risk-contagion network construction, and risk measurement indicator construction. Starting from market multivariate data, the first layer contagion network (based on equity and guarantee) and the second layer contagion network (based on information spillover) from the two-tier network model were found. Theoretically, the debt, equity, and guarantee relationships will constitute a two-way information spillover effect between the two organizations, so in the actual modeling, the second layer network tends to have a higher nodes degree than the first layer network. Finally, through a series of network topology calculations and network category identification, the systematic risk level of a region can be found and the key risk-contagion nodes identified.

7.3 Regression Model

External risk exposure can be used to measure the risk spillover level from a corporate bankruptcy to the regional economy. From the perspective of macro-prudential supervision, a meaningful question is whether the company's external risk exposure is related to factors such as industry, region, listed company, and ownership. In addition, ERE is based on information in the financial statements, which is a static indicator. It is difficult to reflect the complexity of the actual business activities of a company associated with the socioeconomic system and the systematic importance in the economic system. From the perspective of complex networks, evaluation of the importance of a company in the regional economic system can be identified. From the perspective of risk-contagion networks, it is possible to measure the risk spillover level of a company's bankruptcy in the regional economic system. Thus, regression models can be used to study two problems:

1. What factors are related to external risk exposure, whether it is affected by factors such as industry, region, listed company, and corporate ownership?
2. Whether the company's external risk exposure can cover the indicators in the risk-contagion network?

Multiple linear regressions of risk exposures are obtained using two types of variables, the first type is the complex network measurement indicators such as node degree and clustering coefficient, and the second type is the enterprise's own attributes and financial indicators. The balance of external risk exposure is affected by several factors, the most significant one is the size of a company. In order to rule out the impact of this factor, the three variables, revenue, net asset, and bond balance are used to control the effect of company size.

Besides company size, there is substantial evidence that idiosyncratic company factors affect external risk exposure. Specifically, idiosyncratic factors include ownership, industry, and whether the company is listed or not. After controlling for size, the empirical model is used to examine whether ERE was affected by these idiosyncratic factors.

The structure of the risk-contagion network is the focus of this research. After building an inter-enterprise risk-contagion network, it was found that different nodes have a heterogeneous location and status in this network, which affects the role of enterprises in the risk-contagion process. An important question is whether the role of enterprises in regional risk contagion could be reflected only by the external risk exposure. Whether network analysis can provide a new perspective of risk-contagion analysis? Two indicators, node degrees and local aggregation coefficients, were used to represent the attributes of nodes in the risk-contagion network. Their relationship was clarified with external risk exposure through empirical models.

$$\ln RiskExpo_i = \beta_0 + \sum_{j=1}^{9} \beta_j \cdot x_{ij} + u_i$$

$$\ln RiskExpo_i = \beta_0 + \beta_1 \cdot DegNet_i + \beta_2 \cdot ClusCoef_i + \beta_3 \cdot \ln Reve_i \qquad (7.12)$$
$$+\beta_4 \cdot \ln BondBal_i + \ln \beta_5 \cdot NetAsset_i + \beta_6 \cdot PropFirm_i$$
$$+\beta_7 \cdot Indust_i + \beta_8 \cdot ListedCom_i + \beta_9 \cdot Reg_i$$

where $RiskExpo_i$ is external risk exposure. $DegNet_i$ and $ClusCoef_i$ are nodes degree and clustering coefficient of networks, respectively. $Reve_i$ and $NetAsset_i$ are total revenue and net asset in balance sheets, respectively. $BondBal_i$ is the balance of the company's unpaid bonds. $PropFirm_i$, $Indust_i$, $ListedCom_i$, and Reg_i are dummy variables. $PropFirm_i$ represents the ownership of enterprise i, the value equal to 1 represents a state-owned enterprise while the value equal to 0 represents a private enterprise. $Indust_i$ represents the industry of enterprise i, the value equal to 1 represents manufacturing industry while the value equal to 0 represents service industry. In our sample, manufacturing includes industry, daily consumption, information technology, healthcare and materials; the service industry includes optional consumption and real estate. $ListedCom_i$ represents whether enterprise i is a listed company, the value equal to 1 represents a listed company while the value equal to 0 represents non-listed company. Reg_i represents the location of enterprise i.

ERE is based on information in the financial statements, which is a static indicator. Therefore, the following inferences are drawn: external risk exposure cannot cover node degree, and local clustering coefficient and other indicators are obtained through complex network modeling.

A two-tier counterparty risk-contagion network model is built using four dimensions: concept definition, data structure, risk-contagion network construction, and risk measurement indicator construction. Compared with the existing risk-contagion network model, the proposed model overcomes several shortcomings and is innovative. In terms of concept definition, the model proposed in this paper comprehensively considers various types of risk communication mechanisms and defines risk communication networks in two dimensions: financial channels and information channels. In terms of data structure, the proposed model does not use simulation data in methods such as "maximum entropy", and not only uses financial data, but uses a combination of qualitative and quantitative data sources. The construction of risk-contagion networks is based on innovative work in both conceptual definition and data structure. Finally, in the construction of risk measurement indicators, a new indicator of external risk exposure for empirical analysis is proposed.

7.4 Empirical Study on Nonfinancial Corporate Debt Risk Contagion

From the debt risk analysis of the government, residents, and nonfinancial corporation, it can be seen that the nonfinancial corporation debt accounts for 60% of China's total real economy debt, and the leverage ratio is 151.82%, much higher than the other two departments. The large repayment pressure makes the half of the new credit bond issuance funds used for repayment of interest in the current year. Therefore, this paper will focus on the debt risk of the nonfinancial corporate sector and analyze the potential systematic risk issues in the nonfinancial corporate sector through a regional sample.

7.4.1 Sample Data

At present, small- and medium-sized bond issuers are facing difficulties in financing. Some enterprises in Shandong, Jiangsu, Fujian, and other regions have adopted mutual guarantees and joint guarantees to improve credit qualifications and facilitate financing. This has led to the development of systematic risk management practices with Chinese characteristics. In order to obtain higher bond issuance quotas or lower financing costs, small and medium enterprises (SMEs) use mutual guarantees and joint guarantees to help their financing, which makes the interfirm guarantee relationship and equity relationship between enterprises intertwined, and it is easy to form the regional risk-contagion network.

The credit bond guarantee circle network often has a strong regional character. This regionality is reflected in two aspects. First, the scale and characteristics of the external guarantees of issuers in different regions are often different. The average external guarantee ratio between different provinces varies above 30%. In some provinces, industrial bond issuers have a high proportion of external guarantees, and some provinces have a high proportion of external guarantees. Second, due to the "acquaintance society"—the origin of the guarantee circle, the guarantee circle is often confined to a certain area. The guarantee circle originated from the "acquaintance society". For industrial bonds, the guarantee network usually originated from the same industry in the same region, or the owner of the upstream and downstream industries. For city investment bonds' issuers, the guarantee objects are mostly under the control of the same State-owned Assets Supervision and Administration

Table 7.1 Top 5 provinces of credit bond and bank loan scale

Province	Guang Dong	Jiang Su	Zhe Jiang	Shan Dong	Bei Jing
Bank credit	79302.41	78488.50	62698.98	50507.64	50042.80
Credit bond	42915.41	40681.62	29416.02	25516.06	252609.18

Table 7.2 Statistics on the external guarantee ratio of bond issuers

Province	External guarantee ratio (%)	Province	External guarantee ratio (%)
Jiang Su	37.49	Chong Qin	14.42
Zhe Jiang	31.99	Fu Jian	13.60
Tian Jing	23.80	Gui Zhou	13.50
Qing Hai	23.23	Ji Lin	12.77
Xi Zang	22.68	He Bei	11.42
Shan xi	22.48	Xin Jiang	11.33
Shan dong	19.58	Nei Meng	11.23
He Nan	18.42	Yun Nan	10.80
Bei Jing	18.19	Hu Bei	10.75
Si Chuan	15.66	Shang Hai	10.28
An Hui	14.56	Jiang Xi	9.57

Commission of the State Council (SASAC), or the city investment platform of the neighboring city.

The regional nature of the credit bond guarantee circle indicates that empirical analysis in a certain region is appropriate. However, if the sample is confined to a city, the guarantee network cannot be fully developed, and the representativeness of its network structure is not strong enough. Therefore, the guarantee network in a province is constructed.

The scale of nonfinancial corporate debt in each province was considered, including credit bonds and loans. The provinces with large debts have systemic importance in the process of debt risk identification, control, and prevention. Nonfinancial corporate debt can be divided into direct financing debt and indirect financing debt. The former is mainly credit bond financing, and the latter is mainly bank credit. The bank credit and credit bond market data as of December 2018, which were provided by The People's Bank Of China, are shown in Table 7.1. The nonfinancial corporate debts in Guangdong and Jiangsu are among the top two.

The risk-infected network proposed in our paper incorporates information on external guarantees between enterprises, and it is reasonable to use the provinces with a higher proportion of external guarantees as samples. "External guarantee/net assets" were used to describe the proportion of external guarantees issued by credit bond issuers. The results of the provinces are shown in Table 7.2, data are from wind, as of December 2017. Judging from the proportion of external guarantees issued by credit bond issuers, Jiangsu and Zhejiang rank among the top two.

Based on the information in Tables 7.1 and 7.2, you can see that nonfinancial corporations in Jiangsu Province have two characteristics: large debt scale and high external guarantee ratio. Further, Jiangsu's GDP in 2018 ranks second among the all provinces in China and is an important economic engine in the Yangtze River Delta. From the perspective of economic scale, the real economic sector of Jiangsu Province has an outstanding position in China's economic system. With strong systemic importance, comprehensive debt scale, external guarantee ratio, and economic volume, this paper selects Jiangsu Province as the sample selection area.

China's credit bond market can be divided into industrial bonds and city investment bonds. Our work chooses industrial bond issuers as research objects. There are two main reasons: first, non-city investment platform debt accounts for about 78% of nonfinancial corporate debt, and city investment platform debt only accounts for 22%; up to now, default enterprises are all industrial bond issuers. Second, the issuer of city investment bonds has a certain gap with the industrial bond issuer in the authenticity, completeness, and availability of information disclosure. The annual report, audit report, and prospectus and other information of industrial bond issuer not only follow the regular disclosure process, but the content is more realistic. Relatively speaking, the city investment platform has more irregular expressions in the information disclosed regularly, and the contents of the financial statements are not detailed. Therefore, in the subject of research, increasing the proportion of industrial bond issuers will help improve the availability of data and data quality. From the above two points, the industrial bond issuers can be mapped to the majority of the nonfinancial corporate sector debt (78%), while taking into account the data quality. In the end, the financing guarantee circle of Jiangsu industrial bond issuer was selected as the research object.

7.4.2   Construction of the First Layer Network

The first-tier counterparty network of industrial bond issuer guarantee circles in Jiangsu Province was established. Data were collected from 518 credit bond issuers in Jiangsu Province as of September 2018 as the main node samples. The companies covered by the whole network include provincial bond issuers related to the main nodes through the guarantee relationship and equity relationship. Among them, there are 330 main nodes in the city investment platform and 188 major industrial bond issuers. The external guarantee relationship of all enterprises uses the latest external guarantee information disclosed by the company in the third quarter of 2018 and does not include the historical information of the company's external guarantee. All corporate financial data are based on financial data for the third quarter of 2018. All data come from wind.

The intent is to build a network based on the real regional credit bond guarantee information. The construction of the actual network is divided into the following steps. First, selecting 188 major industrial bond issuers in the overall sample. Second, collecting data for each bond issuer, including external guarantees, acceptance of guarantees and equity relationships, ending in the third quarter of 2018. Last, according to the above relationship, setting the issuer as the node, using guarantee and equity relationship as the edges, then a directed network is

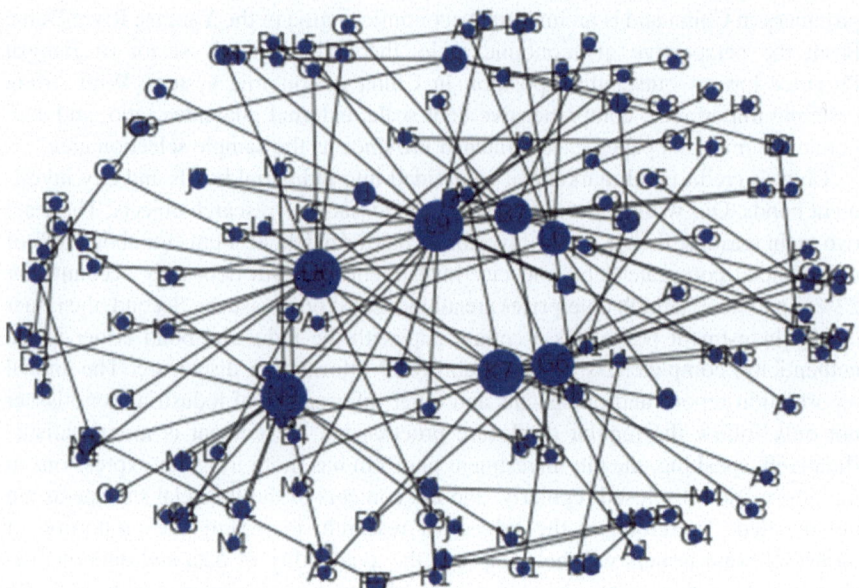

Fig. 7.1 The first network of industrial bond issuers in Jiangsu province

constructed. In the network graph, each node corresponds to a credit bond issuer. Serial numbers "A1, A2, B1, ..., Z9" were used to randomly mark the issuer's enterprise. In the construction of the network, some of the nodes connected to A1 may not bond issuers. For non-bond issuer companies, such as A2, the following treatment was applied. If A2 can establish the above connection with the second issuer enterprise B1 in the network, it will be kept in the network; otherwise, the network will be removed. This is because, when A2 can be connected to B1, it completes the connection between A1 and B1 as an intermediate bridge, that is, a path as a risk-contagion channel between A1 and B1.

Figure 7.1 shows the first-level risk-contagion network of Jiangsu industrial bond issuers. In the figure, the few points and edges independent of the main network were eliminated to obtain the Giant Component. The node size in this network is weighted by node degrees. It can be seen from the figure that after the enterprises with large bond balance in Jiangsu Province are found out, they can form a large-scale network structure through the connection of the guarantee relationship and the equity relationship. From this initially constructed network, the following characteristics can be observed: First, although the industrial bond issuers are located in different cities and counties in the province, belong to different industries, but most of they can connect with each other through guarantee and equity relationship. Second, in this network, there are some nodes, such as G6, L6, K7, L9, N9, B7, D6, etc. These nodes are connected with many surrounding nodes, but most of the other nodes are only associated with a small number of nodes. Third, this network has a distinctly high

Table 7.3 Statistics of G_h

Node Number	Edges	Average path length	Clustering coefficient	Between centrality not equal to 0
135	128	4.4295	0.0448	11

degree of local clustering. In smaller subnetworks, two-way or ring-shaped edges can be seen, which is the mutual security and joint security phenomenon.

As can be seen from Table 7.3, the first layer network has 135 nodes and 128 edges, and the average shortest path is 4.4295. The between centrality of a node equal to 0 means that all the shortest paths do not pass this node. There are 11 nodes not equal to 0, which means that 11 issuers in the network are in the relative core position, which is the key node of the risk-contagion path in the network.

The categories to which the complex network G_h belongs can be divided by graphical observation and network statistics in Table 7.3. Figure 7.1 shows that the overall connectivity of the first layer network is not high, many nodes are only connected to a nearby core node, and the network has the property of local clustering, it is presented around several nodes such as G6, L6, K7, L9, N9, B7, and D6. The number of connected edges of these core nodes is much higher than other nodes, which is consistent with this feature of scale-free networks. A few nodes in a scale-free network have a number of connections far beyond the average node. These nodes are labeled Hub nodes. The state of the Hub nodes directly determines whether the entire network system can operate normally. A few nodes in the network G_h have degrees far beyond other nodes. Figure 7.2 shows the degree distribution of G_h, it can be seen that the degree distribution of the network significantly matches the characteristics of the power-law distribution.

The most important difference between a scale-free network and other networks (random network and small-world network) is that the former can describe the growth of the network and the preference connection mechanism of the new node. When the new nodes access to network, there is a characteristic of preferential connection to original hub node (more connected edges). From the statistical characteristics, the degree distribution of the scale-free network obeys the power-law distribution, and the average shortest path length is small and the clustering coefficient is high. At the same time, according to the network statistics in Table 7.3, it can be considered that the G_h network has certain characteristics of a scale-free network.

7.4.3 Construction of the Second Layer Network

The second level is based on the interconnection of information between enterprises to establish a network. The information exchange between enterprises has the following meanings: When a private enterprise has a credit event, the credit level of other enterprises owned by the same actual controller will be affected. When a certain enterprise in a certain industry has a credit event, the credit level of other

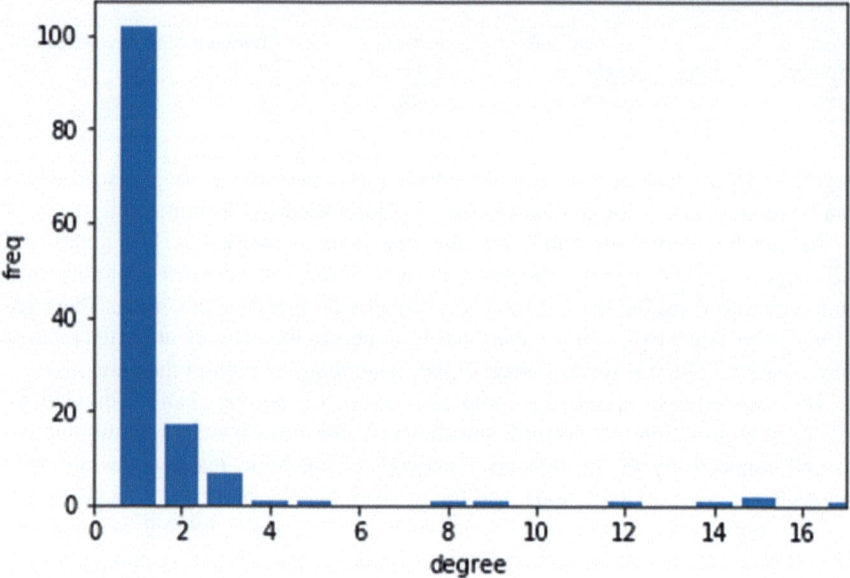

Fig. 7.2 Histogram of network degree distribution in the first layer

enterprises in the same industry in the same region will be affected. Those city investment platforms which under the same local SASAC or the Finance Bureau have a certain degree of information interconnection. For enterprises with guarantee relationships, there is information interconnection between them; for enterprises that are major suppliers or downstream customers, there is an information interconnection relationship between them. Based on the above principles, second layer of information interconnection network between the same nodes as the previous section was constructed. Since the direct information association between the two nodes i and j must be bidirectional, the information interconnection network at this level is an undirected and unweighted network.

Thus, an information internetwork G_m can be constructed:

After the design of the information interconnection mechanism, a second layer information network was constructed. The node size in this network is weighted by node degrees. From Fig. 7.3, the following points can be observed: Firstly, compared with the graph G_m, the overall connectivity of the G_h network is significantly enhanced, the maximum path length is significantly reduced, and the small-world characteristics of the network are initially displayed. Secondly, the network still has a strong regional clustering effect, and several subnetworks can still be found from G_h. Some small-scale inter-enterprise information networks are still the basis of network G_m. By further analyzing the subnetworks, direct information transmission between enterprises in the same industry chain in the same region is common. Finally, the number of key nodes in G_m has increased, and the difficulty of differentiation is higher than that of G_h.

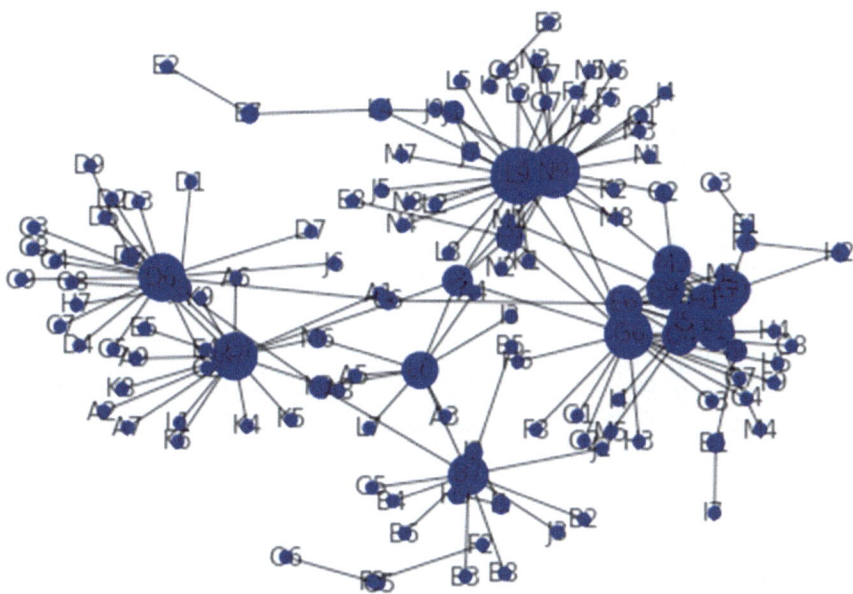

Fig. 7.3 The second layer of information internet

Table 7.4 Statistics of G_m

Node number	Edges	Average path length	Clustering coefficient	Between centrality not equal to 0
135	169	6.5262	0.1142	30

Based on this, the complex network statistics of G_m can be calculated.

Table 7.4 shows that this layer network has 135 nodes, but the number of edges of the network rises to 169. Compared with the Between Centrality of G_h, the number of key nodes in G_m has risen to 30. In general, the increase in the number of key nodes means that the channels of risk contagion are more diverse, but it may also lead to an increase in the stability of the network structure.

Figure 7.4 gives the degree distribution of G_m. The degree distribution of this network also has the characteristic of power-law distribution. However, combined with the significant increase of the clustering coefficient, the average shortest path length in the network drops significantly. G_m has some characteristics of the small-world network, and it should belong to the scale-free plus small-world complex network.

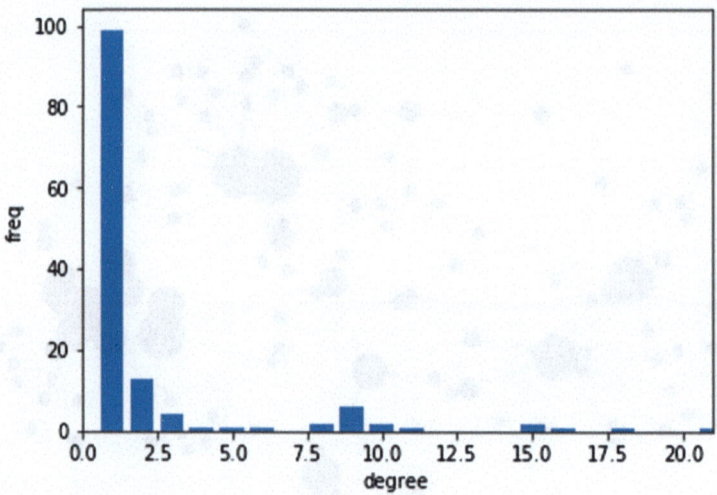

Fig. 7.4 Histogram of network degree distribution in the second layer

7.4.4 Identify Key Risk-Contagion Nodes

External risk exposure of each node was calculated and the G_h and G_m networks reconstructed with risk exposure as the weight, and compared it with the network graph in the previous section.

Figure 7.5 displays the G_h weighted nodes size by external risk exposure. Compared to the G_h weighted nodes size by nodes degree in Fig. 7.3, the position of the biggest nodes has changed. In Fig. 7.1, K7, L9, and D6 are the biggest nodes; it means there are extensive equity and guarantee relationships between these nodes and other enterprises. That is to say, there are extensive micro-risk-contagion channels around these nodes; they are the key nodes in risk-contagion network. However, if node size is weighted by the total potential infection intensity (external risk exposure), different results are obtained. In Fig. 7.5, except for L9, which is still the largest node, the nodes such as K7 and D6 are no longer significant. They are replaced by I1 and E9, which become the nodes with the greatest potential risk contagion.

Figure 7.6 shows the information interconnection network G_m weight nodes size by external risk exposure. Compared with Fig. 7.3, the same conclusion can be drawn, that is, the key risk nodes are measured from the perspective of the micro-risk-contagion channel and the potential infection intensity, which will yield different results.

In fact, through the number of potential micro-risk-contagion channels (node degree) around a specific node, it can be seen how many affiliates will be affected when an enterprise goes bankrupt or default, which is an important indicator to measure the potential systematic risk contribution of this enterprise. The external risk exposure can measure the intensity of risk contagion; it is also an important

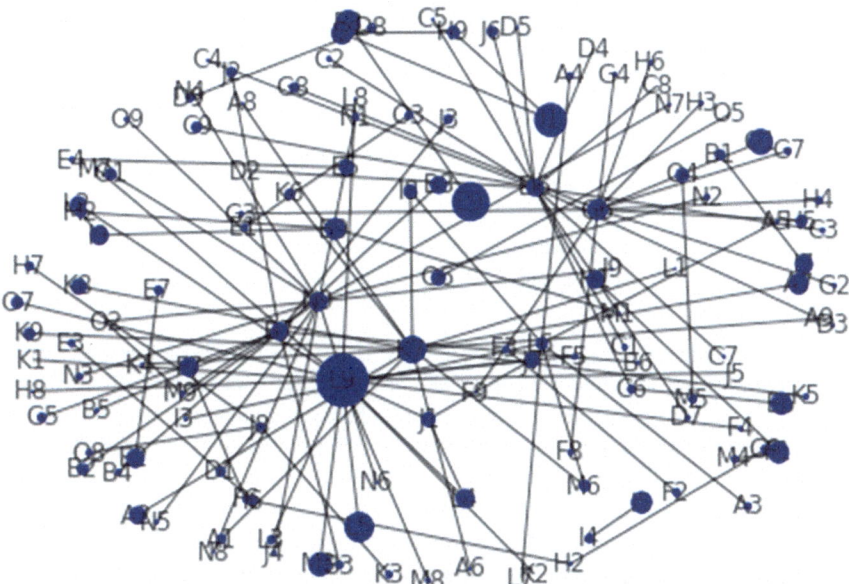

Fig. 7.5 Network diagram of G_h after assigning weight according to ERE

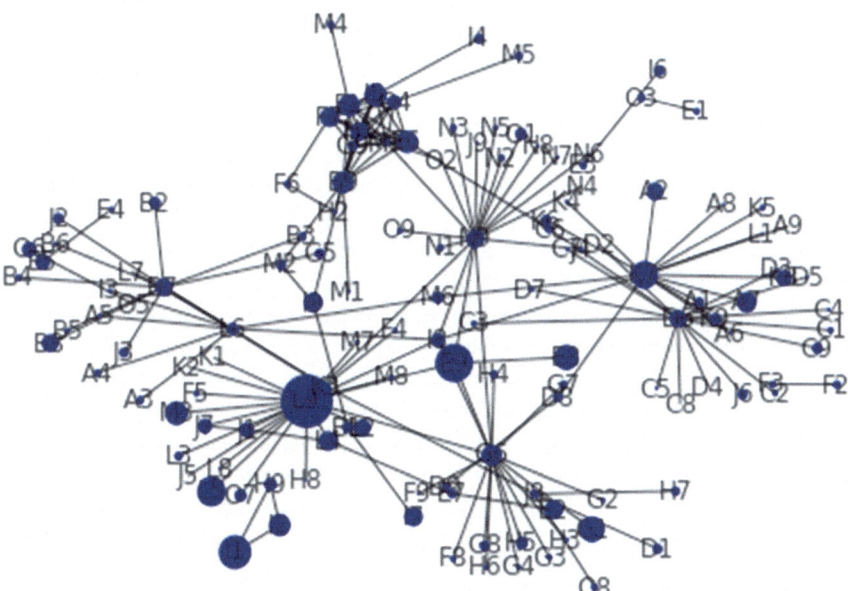

Fig. 7.6 Network diagram of G_m after assigning weight according to ERE

Table 7.5 Some core nodes correspond to enterprises

Node code	Underlying enterprise	Group company?
B7	Xuzhou Construction Machinery Group Co., Ltd	Yes
D6	Wuxi Industry Development Group Co., Ltd	Yes
E9	Suning Electrical Appliance Group Co., Ltd	Yes
I1	Pulp & Paper Industry (China) Investment Co., Ltd	Yes
K7	Jiangsu Shagang Group Co., Ltd	Yes
L9	Jiangsu Communications Holding Co., Ltd	Yes
N9	Phoenix Publishing & Media Group Co., L-td	Yes

indicator to measure the potential systematic risk contribution of this enterprise. When judging the key nodes in the risk-contagion network, these two variables should be integrated to generate a more comprehensive indicator.

After identifying the key risk-contagion nodes in the network through the indicators of the two dimensions of node centrality and external risk exposure, nodes such as B7, D6, E9, G6, I1, K7, L6, L9, and N9 were obtained. A meaningful question is what commonalities exist in such enterprise nodes. Obviously, if common attributes of these core nodes could be identified, it will be beneficial to the management and control of debt risk of nonfinancial corporation.

From Figs. 7.3 and 7.6, there are a series of subnetworks centered on nodes such as B7, D6, E9, K7, L9, and N9. Based on this, it can be speculated that these key nodes should be some important, regionally influential investment and financing groups. The correspondence between the node and the actual enterprise confirms our speculation.

Table 7.5 shows that the core nodes in the network are often the parent companies of large manufacturing groups. Compared with other companies in the group, these parent companies are intragroup investment platforms with many subsidiaries and grandchildren. They usually have better credit ratings and lower financing costs in the financial market, so they are the main financing entities within the group. Due to their high credit ratings and better ability to allocate funds, they are responsible for the large amount of interest-bearing debts guarantee of companies within and outside the group. The parent companies of such enterprise groups usually have large-scale fund allocation capabilities and better external financing capabilities (higher credit ratings) than other companies in the group. However, when a local risk event breaks out, as an intermediary with the financial and credit transactions of the internal and external enterprises of the group, the micro-path of risk contagion is more extensive (higher node center degree); once a credit event occurs, it will often causing a broader risk shock.

7.4.5 Ownership and External Guarantee Scale

According to the previous analysis, small- and medium-sized bond issuers are facing difficulties in financing. Some enterprises in some regions have adopted mutual guarantees and joint guarantees to increase credit rating for each other in order to facilitate their financing process. In China, the financing environment faced by private enterprises and state-owned enterprises is different. In general, state-owned enterprises benefit from the government's implicit endorsement and high social visibility, which has a more relaxed external financing environment than private enterprises. Therefore, the use of mutual insurance and joint insurance to seek external financing opportunities, in more cases, is the passive choice of private enterprises. Enterprises were divided into state-owned enterprises and private enterprises, and verify this phenomenon by comparing the scale of external guarantees with total assets, registered capital, and external risk exposure.

As shown in Table 7.6, the proportion of external guarantees between state-owned enterprises and private enterprises varies widely. On average, the external guarantees/registered capital of private enterprises account for twice as much as state-owned enterprises, and the ratio of external guarantees to owner's equity and external exposure are also significantly higher than those of state-owned enterprises. This empirical result is consistent with the theoretical analysis of this paper.

7.4.6 Determinants of External Risk Exposure

External risk exposure can be used to measure the risk spillover level of a corporate bankruptcy to the regional economy. From the perspective of macro-prudential supervision, a meaningful question is whether the company's external risk exposure is related to factors such as industry, region, listed company, and ownership. In addition, this indicator is based on information in the financial statements, which is a static indicator. It is difficult to reflect the complexity of the actual business activities of a company associated with the socioeconomic system and the systematic importance in the economic system. From the comparison between Figs. 7.3 and 7.6, it can be found that the obtained key risk-contagion nodes are not identical by using external risk exposure and node degree as weights. Solutions to two problems were obtained through a set of regression models:

Table 7.6 Corporate ownership and external guarantee ratio

Ownership	External guarantee/ registered capital (%)	External guarantee/ owner's equity (%)	External guarantee/ external exposure (%)
Private	342.35	20.69	25.77
State-owned	152.92	16.28	15.70

Table 7.7 The results of the regression on risk exposure

Dependent variable	Risk exposure					
	Model 1	Model 2	Model 3	Model 4	Model 5	Model 6
Constant	13.822***	8.653***	8.790***	7.715***	7.713***	7.745***
	(0.346)	(1.216)	(0.931)	(1.150)	(1.161)	(1.242)
Degree	0.022	−0.004	0.004	0.002	0.006	0.004
	(0.035)	(0.029)	(0.024)	(0.023)	(0.027)	(0.020)
Clustering coefficient	84.815	−6.324			−35.514	
	(149.51)	(123.45)			(112.33)	
Revenue		0.302***	0.491***	0.431***	0.496***	0.494***
		(0.082)	(0.078)	(0.698)	(0.081)	(0.078)
Bond balance		0.062*				
		(0.034)				
Net assets		0.055				
		(0.062)				
Property of firm				0.430	0.443	0.429
				(0.277)	(0.283)	(0.303)
Industry			−0.474*	−0.493*	−0.495*	−0.511**
			(0.271)	(0.267)	(0.269)	(0.248)
Listed company			−1.079***	−1.058***	−1.065***	−1.054***
			(0.310)	(0.306)	(0.310)	(0.375)
Region						−0.084
						(0.267)
Controls	No	Yes	Yes	Yes	Yes	Yes
R-squared	0.03	0.39	0.49	0.51	0.52	0.52
Adj R-squared	−0.009	0.33	0.45	0.46	0.45	0.45

1. What factors are related to external risk exposure? Is it affected by factors such as industry, region, listed company, and corporate ownership?
2. Does a company's external risk exposure can cover the indicators in the risk-contagion network?

Reve$_i$ and *NetAsset$_i$* is total revenue in balance sheets. *BondBal$_i$* is the balance of the company's unpaid bonds. Model 2 is used to compare the effects of the three control variables. It was found that revenue can control the size of the company effectively. In models 3, 4, 5, and 6, revenue was used as the control variable.

The results of the regression are as follows:

Table 7.7 displays the resulting regression models. In model 1, node degree and local clustering coefficient were used, obtained from risk-contagion network, as independent variables to regress the external risk exposure. These two independent variables in Model 1 are not significant, and the R-squared is close to zero. This leads to a preliminary judgment that external risk exposure cannot cover the indicators in the risk-contagion network. The external risk exposure of enterprises has a positive relationship with the enterprise size. Revenue, net assets, and bond balance were chosen as the control variables of enterprise size. Model 2 was used to screen the control variables of enterprise size, and revenue were found to be the best controlling variables for enterprise size. After controlling the enterprise size, model 3 indicated that the external risk exposure is related to the industry and whether it is listed. The coefficient of *Indust* is negative, indicating that after controlling other factors, the average external risk exposure of manufacturing enterprises is lower than that of service enterprises. The coefficient of *ListedCom* is negative, indicating that after controlling for other factors, the average external exposure of the listed company is lower than that of the non-listed company. This may be due to the high threshold of listed companies in China, and the higher regulatory make listed companies more stringent in external risk management. Through models 4/5/6, *Indust* and *ListedCom* are always significant, but *PropFirm* and *Reg* are not significant. This result indicates that ownership and location are not the main determinants of external risk exposure. Through model 3/4/5/6, the coefficients of $DegNet_i$ and $ClusCoef_i$ are not significant. These empirical results confirm our inferences in the previous paragraph, external risk exposure, which is a static indicator, cannot cover all the information of corporate's external risk spillover effects. From the perspective of complex networks, it has great significance to build an inter-enterprise risk-contagion network. It is also consistent with the conclusions obtained in the previous comparison between Figs. 7.3 and 7.6. From the perspectives of complex network topology and external risk exposure, the identified key risk-contagion enterprises are not completely consistent. Two types of indicators should be combined to find those enterprises with systemic importance.

7.5 Inferences

The credit bond market not only has the individual risk of a single bond but is also a potential source of systematic risk. Specifically, bond issuers have mutual guarantees and joint guarantees for each other's debt, there are equity relations and transaction relationships between issuers, companies in the same geographical region and same industry are clearly relevant in the credit level, and so on. When issuers form a guarantee circle through those guaranty relationship, local risks can spread through this network and become a potential source of systematic risk.

Implications of this study can be recapped in three points:

First, when researching interagency risk-contagion networks, the maximum entropy method is often used to estimate the real interinstitutional risk-contagion path. This paper uses real Financial transactions between enterprises, including guarantees, debts, and equity relationships. This paper also innovatively adds mutual insurance and information spillover risks to the network construction.

Second, this paper constructs a first-tier risk-infected network that only includes financial funds and a second-tier risk-infected network that includes information spillover risks separately. Later, it was found that the information spillover effect could change the risk infection network structure, thereby changing the micro-mechanism of risk contagion and accelerating the transmission of risk.

Third, existing research often uses structural hole theory when identifying systematic financial institutions based on complex networks. This method uses metrics rank the relative importance of the financial institutions directly, and only the network topology attributes are considered. However, after adding external risk exposure to the relative ranking of the importance of the institutions, the results would be more reasonable and effective.

Based on the above theoretical and empirical research, the following four points of recommendations in managing and controlling the risk correlation of nonfinancial corporation are made:

1. The expansion of the regional guarantee circle network should be controlled. External guarantees should be supervised more prudentially than the internal guarantees within the group. Unlike many risk-contagion channels within a group, external guarantee is an important way to make the cross-industry and cross-regional risk contagion.
2. When identifying and supervising key nodes in risk-contagion network, the regulatory authorities should comprehensively consider the indicators of the two dimensions including external risk exposure and external relevance.
3. When the government plans to intervene and control the regional risks of nonfinancial corporation, they should pay more attention to those key nodes, such as the group's investment and financing platform. Theoretical analysis shows that the regional credit bond issuers' guarantee circle is an important contagion path for potential regional systematic risk outbreaks, but external liquidity support can help the system to restore equilibrium. The government can resolve risk spread as soon as possible by coordinating financial institutions to provide external assistance. The existing guarantee network has the topological characteristics of the scale-free network and the connection degree of some nodes far beyond general nodes. Therefore, assistance to the above key nodes can effectively prevent the risk spreading in the system.
4. Prudently supervising disorderly external guarantees of small- and medium-sized issuers. The empirical analysis shows that the key nodes in the network are often the connection hub between one subnetwork and another subnetwork. It is more effective to rescue the key nodes when regional risk events occur. Once such risk-contagion network with scale-free attributes evolves into a random network, contagion mechanism will be more diverse, and the efficiency of external assistance will drop significantly.

7.6   Conclusions

Previous studies have shown that small-world Bank network structure with the same number of nodes has the weakest stability in the face of external impact, while the scale-free network structure has the strongest stability. Therefore, it is necessary to prudently supervise the disorderly external guarantees of small- and medium-sized issuers (non-key nodes with less connectivity within the system) and prevent the existing guarantee circle evolve into a random network structure.

References

1. BIS. (2019). *Annual Economic Report*, 2019.
2. Edirisinghe, C., Gupta, A., & Roth, W. (2015). Risk assessment bassed on the analysis of the impact of contagion flow. *Journal of Banking and Finance, 60*, 209–223.
3. Watts, D. J., & Strogatz, S. H. (1998). Collective dynamics of small-world networks. *Nature, 393*, 440–442.

Chapter 8
The Effect of COVID-19 on the Banking Sector

Abstract The COVID-19 pandemic has had a massive impact on the global economy. The impact COVID-19 has had on the Chinese banking sector consists of three aspects: short-term, long-term, and systemic risks. Support for differentiated financial services for pandemic prevention and control is needed, with increased credit support. Medium-to-small enterprises need to be supported through special credit lines, reduced interest rates on loans, deferred repayments, and establishment of long-term credit systems. Digital transformation needs to take place at a faster rate to improve intelligent risk control systems.

COVID-19 has created a very difficult challenge throughout the world. In addition to many illnesses and deaths, large portions of the world population are quarantined or have had their freedom of movement limited. We will win the "war" against COVID-19, but in many aspects, the world will not be the same after COVID-19. One aspect is that we will have a world recession. Unemployment has soared, hopefully temporarily, but this has put a major crimp in the economy. One indication of how the economy in the near future is expected to evolve is the reaction of the world's stock exchanges. They have plummeted, losing about one-third of their value (although they have recovered to a great degree after governments took drastic fiscal action). The changing economic strength of the banks (due to their reduced market value) can have consequences for the rest of the business community because banks have a special role in the financial system and partly because most of all the business transactions take place through banks and partly because the banks are important for financing the reconstruction of the world business community.

In 2019, total profit from Chinese banks reached $312 billion, ranking first in the world, nearly a quarter more than that of US banks. The Industrial and Commercial Bank of China (ICBC) had the highest total profit and net profit and China Construction Bank (CCB) was in the second place. At present, China has brought the pandemic under control through suppression measures and is trying to accelerate the

---

We wish to acknowledge the work of Ying Kang, upon which this chapter is based.

full restoration of production and living order while maintaining pandemic prevention and control. A variety of policies would safeguard the banking system, maintain sufficient liquidity, and promote the development of the real economy. China's economy is stabilizing which contributes to the development of the global industrial chain, which will thus help resist the threat of world recession.

8.1   Short-Term Impacts on Bank Performance Indicators

Short-term credit demand of the residential sector has dropped a great deal, while that of nonfinancial corporations has risen. The pandemic led to people living in isolation, making consumption sluggish, and credit card loans declined remarkably. Personal business loans were difficult to resume because micro- and small business owners return to work facing early repayment to avoid unnecessary interest expenses. The number of short-term household new RMB loans was −¥114.9 billion in January and −¥450.4 billion in February, a year-on-year decrease of ¥407.9 billion and ¥157.2 billion, respectively [1]. As for nonfinancial companies, special relending due to the pandemic and credit granted for pandemic prevention have risen. The pandemic has led to funding pressures for some companies, and corporations with credit have increased withdrawals. As a result, the figure of their short-term new RMB loans was +¥769.9 billion in January and +¥654.9 billion in February, a year-on-year increase of ¥178 billion and ¥506.9 billion, respectively [1].

The service industry and micro, small, and medium-sized enterprises (MSMEs) struggled for survival during this period. Learning from experiences gained from the SARS outbreak of 2003, the most influenced industries were the tertiary, especially transportation, accommodation, and catering (Fig. 8.1). Data sources used to depict figures are from Wind data vendor. By 2018, China's MSMEs accounted for 99.8% of all enterprises [1]. These were mainly labor-intensive and asset-light industries such as wholesale and retail, accommodation, catering and tourism, accounting for more than 70%. In the other direction, demand for credit in the healthcare industries, e.g. the firms producing preventive/protective equipment, has grown. The rising demand for "new consumer" credit, such as online e-commerce, online education, and online office, has partially hedged downward pressure on consumption.

The traditional concept of "early investment and early income" means Chinese bank credit investment follows a "3322" pattern. There is pressure to maintain steady growth, and more supportive governmental policies may be launched for this purpose. Consequently, the credit scale may see a sharp rebound after the pandemic period.

The pandemic situation has had a differential impact on the quality of bank assets. The pandemic has affected China's manufacturing, consumption, and import and export activities. Total retail sales of social consumer goods and gross value of

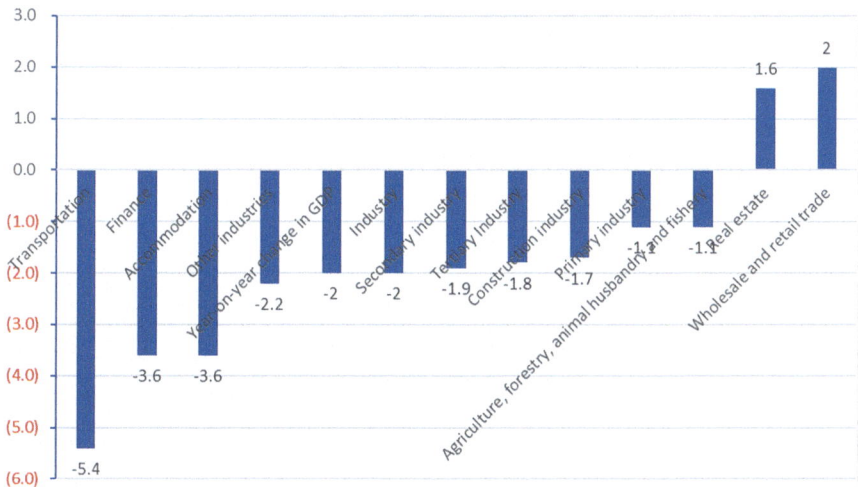

Fig. 8.1 Degree of negative impact on different industries during SARS (%)

imports and exports declined by 38.3%, 20.5%, and 9.6% from January to February, respectively [2]. Under the influence of the pandemic, the nonperforming loan ratio of commercial banks may rise. If the macroeconomy is relatively stable, bank asset quality is expected to remain steady. From a regional perspective, the banks with a higher proportion of credit in Hubei province are more affected, but the impacts are limited overall. As of 2019, the loans of Hubei province accounted for 3.29% of the national total [1]. From the industry perspective, tertiary sector components such as transportation, tourism, catering, and accommodation are more affected by the pandemic, and the pressure on their asset quality is greater. At the end of 2017, the distribution of RMB loans by financial institutions showed that transportation, warehousing, and postal services; wholesale and retail industries; and accommodation and catering industries made up 9.3%, 7.2%, and 0.6% of bank loans, respectively (Fig. 8.2). From the perspective of the group size, MSME cash flow is more easily disrupted, their default risks and asset quality pressure are greater. From the perspective of banks, the pandemic has a little negative impact on the asset quality of state-owned banks and joint-stock banks. However, downward pressure increased on the asset quality of small and medium-sized banks in the short term. The longer the pandemic lasts, the greater pressure on their credit risks. A series of measures have been launched to resolve the problem. The People's Bank of China (PBC) has implemented three reserve requirement ratio (RRR) reductions with a total of ¥1.75 trillion since 2020 [3]. In the meantime, departments will continue to promote the adjustment and optimization of the credit structure and the transformation of operations and businesses.

The net interest margin has narrowed. The impact of the pandemic on net interest margin is mainly reflected in three aspects: First, the cost of bank liabilities increases. The pandemic considerably influences the growth of enterprises and residents'

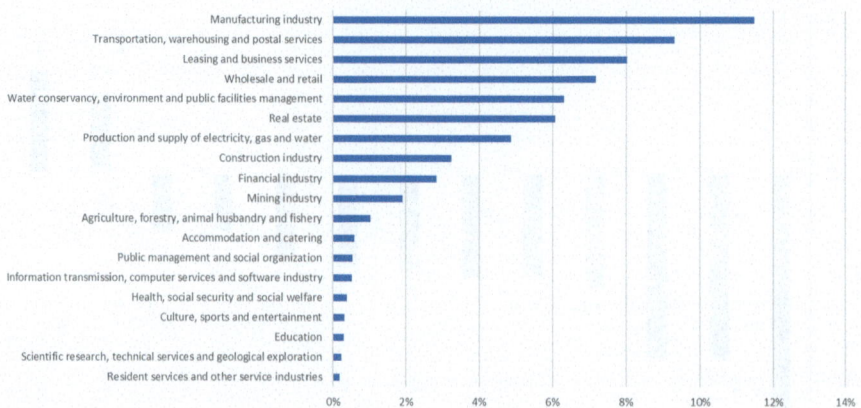

Fig. 8.2 Proportion of bank loans in different types of industries (%)

income and slows down the growth of bank deposits. Second, the short-term loan demand reduction affects bank loan bargaining power and impacts the loan interest rate. Third, the decrease of Loan Prime Rate (LPR) interest rate and other regulatory policies led to the decline of bank lending rates. On February 20, one-year LPR and five-year LPR were 4.05% and 4.75%, a decrease of 10 BP and 5 BP compared with the previous month, respectively. In March, LPR was not adjusted, because it was about the pattern, not about direction. Pattern considerations need to take account of the capabilities of the financial support entities. Due to previous interest rate reduction and relending, the interest rate of credit has fallen remarkably. In February, the interest rate of general loans (excluding personal housing loans) was 5.49%, 0.61% lower than that of July 2019 (before the LPR reform), and the decrease was significantly greater than the 0.26% drop of one-year LPR in the same period [4]. The market expects that in mid-to-late April, Medium-term Lending Facility (MLF) and LPR interest rate are expected to be cut.

8.2   Long-Term Impact on the Banking Industry Is Limited

In the medium term, the influence on the banking industry depends on the future development of the pandemic. Since the end of February, COVID-19 has spread across the world, and the global cumulative number of confirmed cases amounted to 1,605,870 by April 9 (Fig. 8.3). This has had a major impact on the world economy. Under the influence of market sentiment, global financial markets have fluctuated sharply. The banking sector is facing double shocks from the physical economy and financial markets. The pandemic itself is extremely contagious, and the differences in prevention and control strategies and levels make the risk of international cross-over and reciprocal transmission higher. Central banks and financial regulators in various countries and regions around the world have launched various policies to

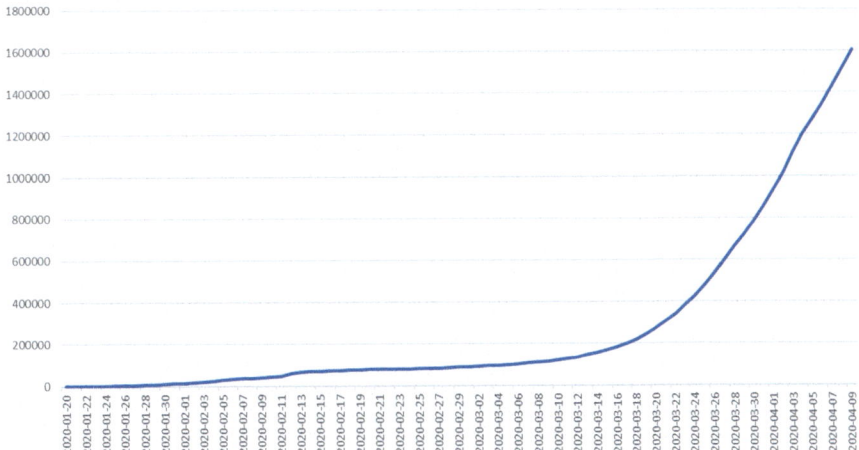

Fig. 8.3 Global cumulative number of confirmed cases of COVID-19

encourage and support the banking sector to actively bolster enterprises and individuals. The Neil Ferguson team from Imperial College estimated that interventions across all 11 countries would have averted 59,000 deaths up to 31 March (claiming a 95% credible interval of 21,000–120,000). They believe that although we are not sure that the existing measures have controlled the pandemic in Europe, we have reason to be optimistic according to current trends.

The first quarter meeting of the Monetary Policy Committee of PBC held that the impact of the COVID-19 on China's economy is generally controllable, China's economic growth remains resilient, and the fundamentals of long-term trend for the better will not change. From the perspective of global macroeconomic patterns, China's economy is relatively stable, and its contribution to the world economy is increasing. In 2018, China's GDP accounted for 15.9% of the world economy, and its nominal GDP reached 66% of that of the United States, making China the world's second-largest economy. Import and export service trade, foreign direct investment, and attracting foreign direct investment ranked second. The number of outbound tourists and overseas tourism expenditure was in the first percentile. In 2019, China's GDP was $14.4 trillion, ranking second in the world, 6.1% higher than the previous year, contributing about 30% to world economic growth.

In 2019, the overall operation and development of China's banking sector was in good shape, and its ability to resist risks was improved. First, the net profit growth of China's large commercial banks reached the highest level in recent years. The net profit of ICBC and CCB rose by 4.9% and 4.8%, respectively, compared with the prior year [1]. Second, at the end of 2019, the loan loss reserve of China's commercial banks was ¥4.49 trillion, an increase of ¥49.2 billion in contrast to the third quarter, and the provision coverage rate and the capital adequacy ratio was 186.08% and 14.64%, respectively [5]. Third, China's banking investment and trading business are mainly concentrated in the bond sector, whose participation in the capital market is far less than that of American and European Banks, so its extent of exposure to market fluctuations is relatively limited.

In order to hedge short-term impact, Chinese policies to stabilize economic growth will be strengthened. First, a loose and flexible monetary policy will continue. PBC has implemented three RRR reduction since 2020. On January 6, it put a comprehensive RRR cut into practice, releasing ¥800 billion of long-term funds [3]. On March 16, it carried out a targeted RRR cut assessment for financial inclusion and released ¥550 billion in long-term funds. On April 3, the targeted RRR reduction for small and medium-sized banks released another ¥400 billion of long-term funds, amounting to ¥1.75 trillion. Meanwhile, the excess deposit reserve interest rate for financial institutions at the central bank was reduced from 0.72% to 0.35% since April 7. Additionally, ¥300 billion of special relending and ¥500 billion of relending and rediscount policy were issued, and an additional ¥1 trillion will be introduced soon. After 7-day and 14-day reverse repurchase rates were reduced by 10 BP, respectively, on February 3, PBC lessened the 7-day reverse repurchase rate by 20 BP on March 30, indicating that monetary policy has entered the stage of intensifying counter-cyclical adjustment.

PBC will continue to take measures to accelerate a decline in loan interest rates, keep liquidity abundant, and bolster the physical economy. First, a variety of monetary policy tools such as RRR reduction will be used, with loans to commercial banks and special treasury bonds when necessary. Second, continuing promotion of LPR reform begun on August 20, 2019. LPR is linked to MLF-based open market operating interest rates, and all new loans issued by banks refer mainly to the LPR interest rate. Third, guiding the banking system to maintain appropriate profits relative to the real economy. Fourth, continue to play the role of the benchmark deposit rate as the "ballast stone" of the entire interest rate system.

There is still room for a proactive fiscal policy. In the first 2 months of 2020, taxes and fees were reduced by ¥402.7 billion in total, with new added taxes and fees cut up to ¥158.9 billion under the tax preferential policies newly introduced in 2020 to support pandemic prevention and control and economic and social development. As of March 21, the central government had allocated ¥25.75 billion for pandemic prevention and control. ¥271.6 billion was used for health expenditure directly related to pandemic prevention and control. On March 27, the Politburo meeting identified four key policies and strengthened macro-policy hedging. First, the fiscal deficit rate was raised, expected to reach 3–3.5%. Second, the issuance of special government bonds was proposed, expected to be used to help small and medium-sized enterprises (SMEs) and to promote consumption. Third, the size of local government special bonds was to be boosted, expected to increase to 4 trillion or so. Fourth, the construction of key projects was to be increased, which would notably raise infrastructure investment. By March 31, ¥1.08 trillion of new special bonds had been issued in China, an increase of 63% over the previous year. In addition, as of April 3, over 30 provinces and cities of China have issued more than ¥5.6 billion in consumer coupons. It is expected that more provinces and cities will issue consumer coupons in the form of local financial subsidies.

8.3 Pandemic Possibly Increases Systemic Risks in the Banking Industry

Corporate loans account for a large proportion of bank loans. The specific impact depends on the region and the structure of banks' credit, and the enterprises' cash flow. From the perspective of the industry, the higher the proportion of tertiary industry credit that is affected by the pandemic, the higher the risk faced by the banks. Figure 8.4 shows the loan structure of 40 Chinese listed banks' corporate loans. Transportation, warehousing, and postal services account for a relatively high proportion of credit in state-owned banks, while wholesale and retail and manufacturing industries make up a relatively large proportion of small and medium-sized banks' loans [1]. Moreover, rural commercial banks primarily serve MSMEs, and such enterprises have a weak ability to resist risks during the pandemic, so the banking industry faces increased systemic risks spillover from the substantial economy.

Personal loan business is less affected by the pandemic than that of corporate loans. This is because retail business is less affected by fluctuations in the business cycle. The pandemic has a small impact on personal housing loans and consumer loans and a large impact on the operation of individual industrial and commercial households. Personal business loans are greatly affected, but the actual impact depends on the cash flow situation of individual customers. According to the subdivided structure of personal loans of 48 listed banks presented in Fig. 8.5, the proportion of personal housing loans of state-owned banks is relatively high, and the consumption and operating loans of urban commercial banks and rural commercial banks are relatively high (Wind database). Large banks are less affected by the pandemic, while small and medium-sized banks face greater risks, and their contagious risks to large banks will increase.

8.4 Discussions and Suggestions

The following suggestions may reinforce the effort to stabilize the economy and reduce the risk faced by Chinese banks.

First, support for differentiated financial services and establishment of special funds for pandemic prevention and control is called for. Increased credit support for areas badly affected by the pandemic, key industries, and enterprises related to pandemic prevention is needed. Implementation of a differential preferential interest rate loan approval mechanism is needed.

For example, the four major banks (ICBC, CCB, Agricultural Bank of China, and Bank of China) have successively established special funds for pandemic prevention

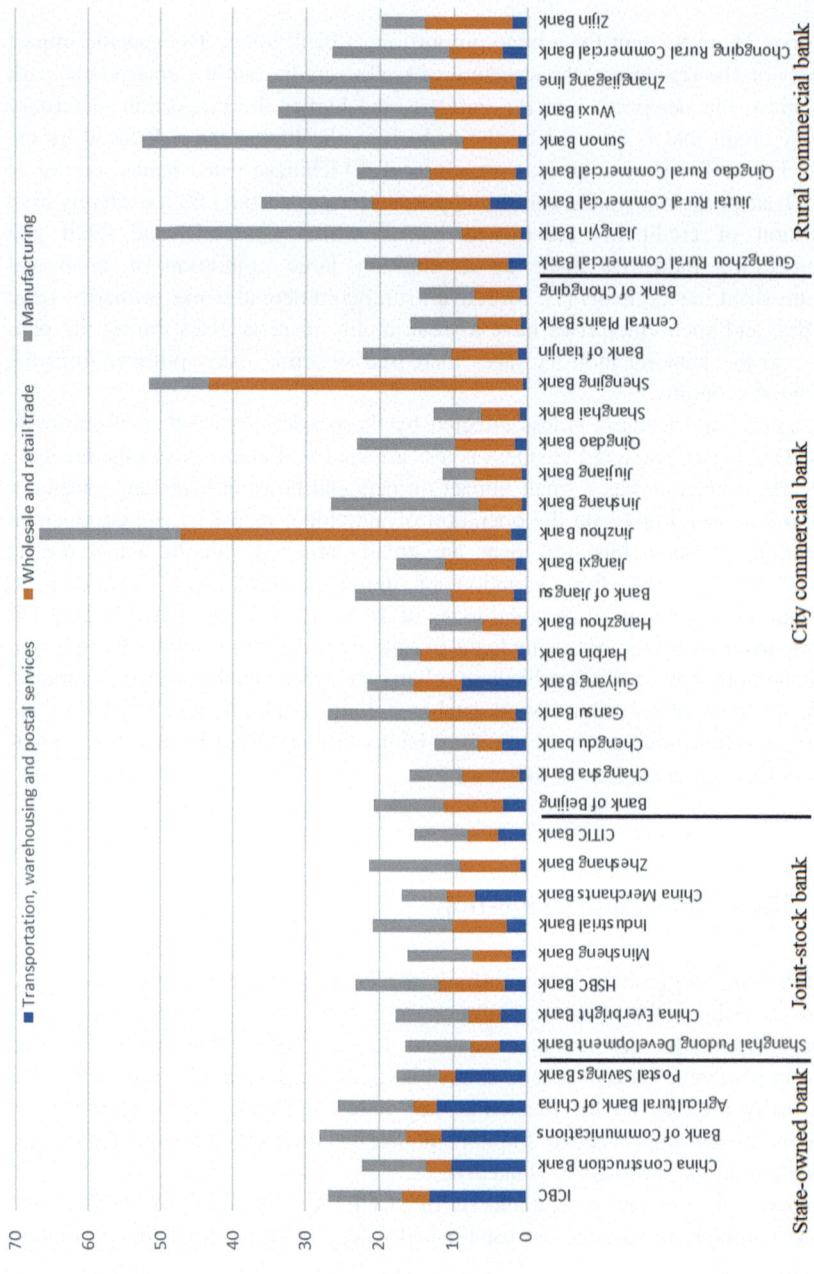

Fig. 8.4 Proportion of credit contribution of the three major industries in total loans (2019H1) (%)

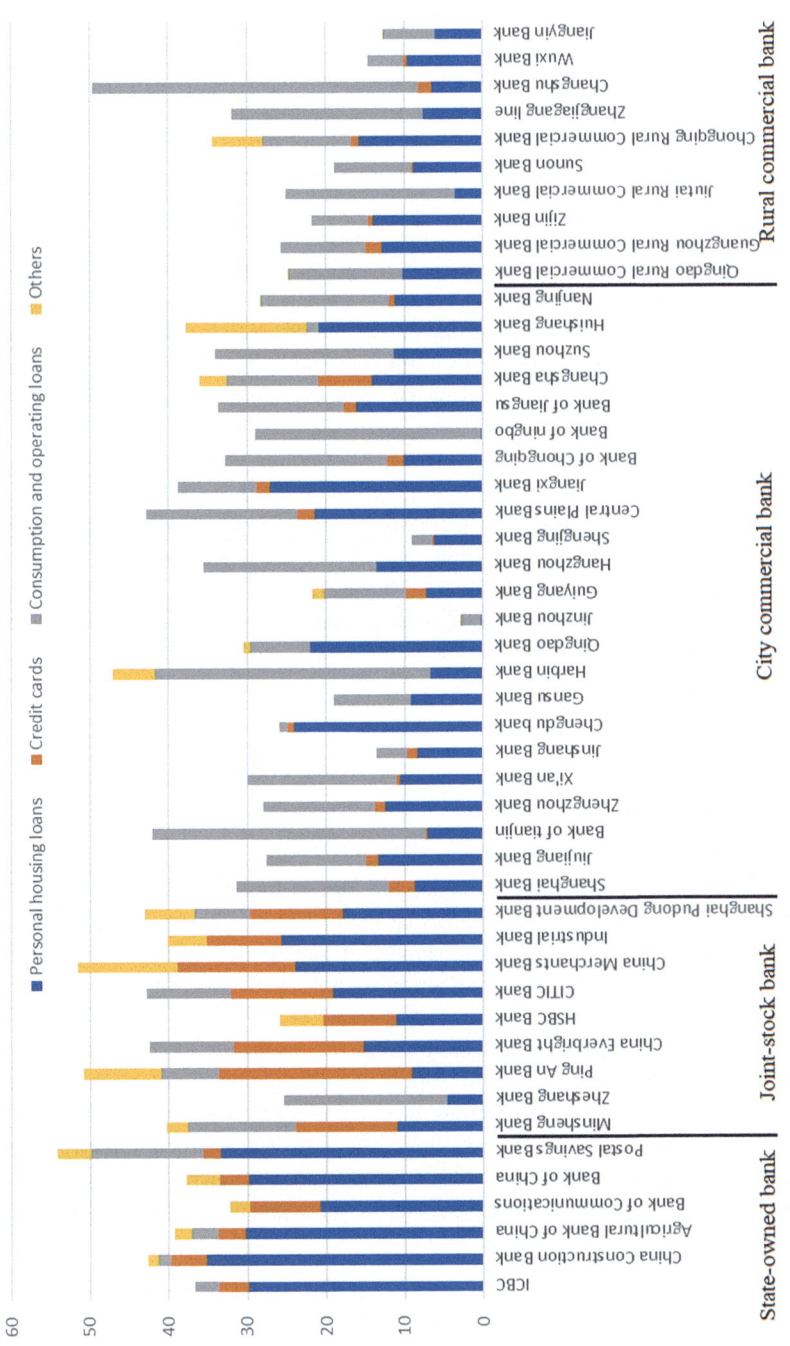

Fig. 8.5 Proportion of subdivision of personal loan in total loans (2019H1) (%)

and control, with more than ¥14 billion to support the enterprises through investment and loan linkages and promote the steady development of the real economy.

Second, MSMEs need to be supported by increasing special credit lines and special credit debt, reducing loan interest rates, deferring repayments, and establish long-term systems. Efficient and accurate fiscal policies need to be implemented, multilevel financial markets established, adjustment of debt structure and the leverage ratio of different departments, financing models changed, and a complete process risk management system established.

On March 2, China Banking and Insurance Regulatory Commission announced that for MSMEs in difficulty, the principal and interest of loans expired since January 25 shall be given temporary deferred principal repayment arrangements for a certain period of time according to the application for deferred principal repayment by the enterprise. This is in combination with the impact of the pandemic situation and the operating conditions of the enterprise by means of loan extension and renewal.

Third, digital transformation and differentiated competition need to take place faster. Full use of big data, cloud computing, artificial intelligence, block-chain, and other technical means is needed to increase the pace of digital transformation of banks and integrate online and offline operations. Data sharing among banks, governments, industry chains, and relative departments needs to be established to strengthen the internal risk control of banks, focus on risk spillovers of system-important industries and system-fragile industries to the banking industry, and improve intelligent risk control system.

8.5   Conclusions

During pandemics, COVID-19 experience has shown that medium-to-small enterprises need to be supported through special credit lines, reduced interest rates on loans, deferred repayments, and establishment of long-term credit systems. Digital transformation needs to take place at a faster rate to improve intelligent risk control systems.

Block-chain technology has proven a useful secure means to conduct business over the cloud. On February 7, an SME supply chain financial service platform based on block-chain was launched in Beijing to overcome problems in their financing. Through block-chain technology, government and the state-owned enterprise procurement contract receivables are confirmed, and various financial resources such as financing guarantees and asset management are aggregated to provide SMEs with comprehensive supply chain financial services.

References

1. Wind database—Comprehensive database on China's fixed income markets.
2. www.stats.gov.cn
3. www.pbc.gov.cn
4. xw.sinoins.com.gov.cn
5. www.cbirc.gov.cn

Chapter 9
Assessment of Smart Healthcare Services

Abstract This chapter considers organizational adoption of smart healthcare services. Pandemic planning would benefit from accessing some of the many technology systems available to aid in operations and planning. A technical acceptance model is adopted as a means to consider factors important in the adoption of technology. Chinese doctors were surveyed to gain attitudes and perceptions of usefulness of healthcare technology. Perceived usefulness and experience were found to be important in intention to adopt healthcare systems.

There are many useful software tools that have been developed to aid healthcare management. Pandemic planning and operations can benefit a great deal with tools that enable quicker organization and development of databases of cases, testing needs, supply needs and locations, etc.

Drawing upon the technical acceptance model (TAM), the basic constructs that affect the practitioners' intentions to adopt smart healthcare services are identified. After that knowledge is obtained, a transfer mechanism is identified as the antecedent of TAM. The moderating impact of the departmental difference on the entire construct is examined. The following sections discuss the theoretical bases and the development of relevant hypotheses.

This chapter draws from Pan, Ding, Wu, S. Yang & J. Yang (2019), Exploring behavioral intentions toward smart healthcare services among medical practitioners: A technology transfer perspective, *International Journal of Production Research* 57 (18), 5801–5820, with permission. That paper includes a full literature review and citation.

9.1   Technology Acceptance Model

9.1.1   Attitude

Davis [1] proposed TAM as an extension of the theory of reasoned action (TRA). According to TRA and TAM, an individual's actual behavior toward certain action is determined by his behavioral intention (BI), which refers to a measure of the strength of his willingness to try and exert while performing a certain behavior. In turn, BI is determined by one's attitude concerning the behavior in question. Attitude refers to the degree of a person's favorable or unfavorable evaluation of the behavior in question. Abundant studies have confirmed that attitude is a determinant of BI [2, 3]. Based on this discussion, we hypothesize:

H1 Attitude has a positive impact on doctors' BI to adopt smart healthcare services.

9.1.2   Perceived Usefulness

Davis explained that an individual's decision to adopt a new technology depends on two beliefs: (1) perceived usefulness (PU) and (2) perceived ease-of-use (PEOU). In the context of this study, PU is defined as the degree to which doctors believe that using smart healthcare services would enhance their job performance. The significant influence of PU on BI has been consistently validated by several studies [4, 5]. In addition, several studies have shown the positive relationship between PU and attitude [2, 6]. Thus, the hypotheses:

H2 PU has a positive impact on doctors' BI to adopt smart healthcare services.

H3 PU has a positive impact on doctors' attitude to adopt smart healthcare services.

9.1.3   Perceived Ease of Use

From the perspective of smart healthcare, PEOU is defined as the degree to which an individual believes that using smart healthcare services would be free of physical and mental effort. PEOU is considered as one of the determinants of attitude. That is, doctors would be more receptive to those convenient and reliable technologies, which could improve work efficiency. Furthermore, previous studies also pointed out that PEOU has a direct impact on PU [2, 7, 8]. Thus, the hypotheses:

H4 PEOU has a positive impact on doctors' attitude to adopt smart healthcare services.

H5 PEOU has a positive impact on PU of smart healthcare services.

9.1.4 Subjective Norm

Subjective norm (SN) is defined as a "person's perception that most people who are important to him think he should or should not perform the behavior in question" [9]. In the original TAM construct, Davis has abandoned the SN of TRA. Dishaw and Strong [10] argued that the abandonment of SN in TAM is debatable, as information technology users will encounter a lot of societal pressure in a social environment, such as stress from supervisors and colleagues. In the context of healthcare, doctors are not completely isolated individuals; they may have a strong BI because of the pressure from superiors or the recommendation from colleagues in the workplace. Physician practices and their sociality lead them to a central position in the healthcare value chain, and they possess a number of unique characteristics, including a strong sense of affiliation with other physicians and potent professional identities that differentiate them from other institutional contexts. Unlike employees in typical work settings, doctors operate with considerably more autonomy and are the ultimate decision makers with regard to patient care. Doctors' interpersonal relationships can persuade themselves to accept new technology, especially when their colleagues have similar or higher status and educational levels. Several studies have already found SN a major contribution on user BI [11, 12]. This study retains the component in the TRA and hypothesizes:

H6 SN has a positive impact on BI to adopt smart healthcare services for doctors.

9.1.5 Perceived Risk

The Valence framework is an important theory that integrates economics with psychology. The framework suggests that consumer perception of the product contains positive PU and negative perceived risk (PR). Bauer [13] first introduced the concept of PR, defined as the uncertainty and the severity of the results. Similarly, physicians' adoption and use of healthcare-related information technologies are also subject to uncertainty and risks. In the context of smart healthcare, doctors may not be willing to try new services if their PR is likely to lead to unpleasant user experience. The findings of previous empirical studies on behaviors with consumers have supported the expectation of a negative relationship between PR and attitude [14, 15]. Thus, the hypothesis:

H7 PR has a negative impact on doctors' attitude to adopt smart healthcare services.

9.2   Technology Transfer

Technology transfer between nonsubstitutable IT products is gradually attracting the interest of researchers because it is a form of usage behavior that is not explored thoroughly in information systems. Based on categorization theory [16], an individual's knowledge of a particular product will be stored in a structured form in the memory, and these memories are organized by the perception knowledge of similar and related products. When consumers evaluate new products, they would search for these memories based on the same category of similar products and ultimately make judgments. For instance, a good offline usage experience would actively guide consumers to online service usage. Similarly, in the healthcare sector, due to the lack of direct user experience, doctors' initial impression and acceptance of smart healthcare may be based primarily on previous associated similar products rather than the technology itself.

Healthcare systems have undergone several evolutions before the concept of smart healthcare emerged. Conventional health care systems are designed to react on illness and are optimized to manage illness. Communication and information technologies have facilitated the delivery of medical services at a distance through telemedicine. Telemedicine, ranging from teleconferencing to rural health monitoring, has extended the reach of medical services from high-quality medical centers to understaffed remote villages. The introduction of electronic medical records has turned the health care systems into eHealth, a new paradigm. Developments in sensors and wearable devices create opportunities to provide clinicians and users with tools and environments to gather physiological data over extended periods of time. This emerging concept is known as mHealth. It represents the evolution of eHealth systems from traditional desktop telemedicine platforms to wireless and mobile platform. Recent advances in computational and storage capacity, dramatic increase in the wireless bandwidth, and advances in AI and big data analysis have made it possible to turn existing healthcare systems (e.g., m-health) into a new and ubiquitous concept called smart healthcare. Istepanian and Al-Anzi [17] defined smart healthcare as mHealth 2.0, and they believe that smart healthcare is an extension of mHealth based on AI and machine learning in the era of big data.

Based on the foregoing discussion, we can clearly understand the close relationship between smart healthcare and mHealth. Table 9.1 gives a comparative analysis between smart healthcare and mHealth. In China, most doctors' awareness of mHealth may only involve some mobile medical applications. Mobile phones and handheld computers are used for online inquiry, remote monitoring, and other simple services. Smart healthcare extends those with more intelligent capabilities, such as assisted diagnosis, real-time instruction, and automatic screening. Clearly, there are differences between them in functionality. Moreover, smart healthcare will involve more risks and uncertainties due to various technology and equipment constraints. On the other hand, it is clear that both smart healthcare and mHealth are outcomes of IT development. In particular, AI-driven smart healthcare is a more advanced stage than mHealth. According to Table 9.1, to some extent, they have

Table 9.1 Comparison of smart healthcare and mHealth

	Smart healthcare	mHealth
Government	Improve scientific level of policy decisions	Effectively grasp the online medical market
	Rapid response to public health threats	Solve shortages
Hospitals	Rational allocation of medical care	Advertising
	Medical service classification	Expand brand influence
	Reduce operating costs	
	Improve service quality	
	Ensure service security	
Doctors	Patient health data management	Mobile interrogation
	Assisted diagnosis	Remote interaction with patients
	Share medical knowledge	Doctor community communication
	Continuing education	
	Publish papers	
Patients	Health management	Online consultation
	Proactive disease protection	Appointment registration
	Timely and effective disease treatment	Doctor recommendations based on needs
	Reduced morbidity	Informative asymmetry
Main risk	Key technical risk	Privacy disclosure
	Business model, industry chain risk	
	Privacy disclosure	
	Medical disputes	
Application environment	Mobile, integrated, dynamic real time	Mobile, online
Commercial model	Traditional medical industry chain	Charging model by information services
		e-business platform transfer payment
Target customers	Government, medical institutions, hospitals, doctors, patients	Doctors, patients

similar application domain, business model, and target customer. Therefore, we argue that doctors' initial acceptance of smart healthcare services can be achieved by their pleasant perception of using mHealth. That is, doctors may regard smart healthcare as a similar member of the mHealth category and gain a judgment criterion relying on the experience of using mHealth according to categorization theory [16]. Therefore, the experience of using mHealth would have a direct positive impact on doctors' perception of smart healthcare services.

The use of a certain existing product positively influences the PU and PEOU for new products, and that both PU and PEOU can be transferred from the existing product to a new product. Similarly, we argue that pleasant usage experience of mHealth would enhance doctor's PU and PEOU for smart healthcare services. When a doctor faces more complex or difficult problems, he would be more willing to try new technologies or services. Therefore, we believe that doctors who have used mHealth tend to exhibit higher PU and PEOU for smart healthcare services.

In addition, when deciding whether to use new technology, potential consumers would weigh in the PRs and perceived benefits. PR is an important factor in the user's decision in mobile and network environment. The newness of smart healthcare services would result in doctors' lack of using experience. According to categorization theory, doctors may make judgments on the risk of smart healthcare services based on their experience of using mHealth. Good experience of using mHealth would negatively influence doctors' PR of smart healthcare services. Based on this discussion, the hypotheses are drawn:

H8 Doctors' experience of using mHealth has a positive impact on the PU of smart healthcare services.

H9 Doctors' experience of using mHealth has a positive impact on the PEOU of smart healthcare services.

H10 Doctors' experience of using mHealth has a negative impact on the PR of smart healthcare services.

H11 Doctors' experience of using mHealth has a direct positive impact on the BI to smart healthcare services.

9.3 Department Difference

Previous studies have suggested that statistical characteristics would affect user behavior and are likely to moderate the relationships between the TAM constructs, such as gender, age, and experience [18, 19]. In the context of healthcare, Chang and Hsu [20] introduced occupation as a moderator in a nationwide acceptance of online Patient-Safety Reporting System (PSRS), and confirmed that the relationship between the Unified Theory of Acceptance and Use of Technology (UTAUT) constructs was different among physicians, nurses, and other medical staff. Kingston et al. [21] found that doctors are less willing to report incident events using an online IS than nurses. Gagnon et al. [22] confirmed that perceptions toward the use of EHR vary between a general practitioner and specialist, and significantly influence their BIs. Thus, for clinicians and nonclinicians (e.g., medical technicians) of great differences in specialty, we argue that department difference also plays an important role in affecting practitioners' behavior, which cannot be ignored in the context of smart healthcare.

In general, a patient would experience several stages, including disease screening, diagnosis, treatment, and rehabilitation when he is admitted to the hospital. In this process, practitioners in different departments play a distinct role as they provide different services to the patient. Clinicians recommend treatment plans according to patients' conditions, while medical technicians provide technical support for the

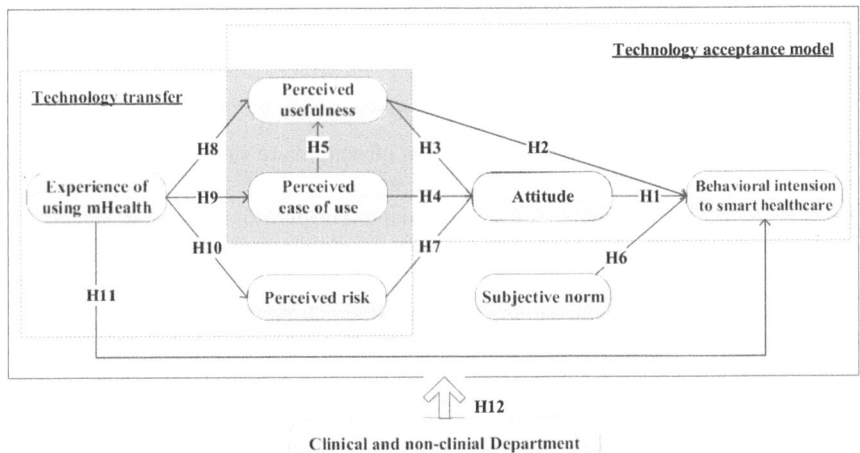

Fig. 9.1 Research framework

clinician's decision. Obviously, clinicians and nonclinicians vary widely in using medical technology. Likewise, the degree and types of risks they are facing also differ. On the one hand, clinicians interact with a large number of patients every day, and their diagnostic results and treatment programs are directly related to the patients' life and health. Therefore, those doctors are more concerned about how to improve efficiency and eliminate errors by using new technologies to assist in medical treatments. On the other hand, for medical technicians who provide services such as B-ultrasound, CT, and pathology, the nature of their daily job is more repetitive than creative. Hence, they are psychologically more hesitant to embrace technical improvements and updates. For example, Rosenkrantz et al. [23] demonstrated the differences between referral physicians and radiologists in their perceptions and user experiences of a "virtual consult" (VC) system. In their study, 80–90% of referral physicians (including emergency medicine, internal medicine, gastroenterology, rheumatology, and general surgery) agreed that VC was easy to use, improved their understanding of radiology reports and patient management. On the other hand, although most radiologists (including abdominal, thoracic, musculoskeletal, neuroradiology, and pediatrics) agreed that VC was easy to use and contributed to patient care, they also expressed a sense of disruption to their normal workflow when using VC. Based on this discussion, the following hypothesis is adopted:

H12   Department difference has a significant moderating impact on each component of the doctors' adoption of smart healthcare services.

Based on these hypotheses, Fig. 9.1 illustrates the interactions between the aforementioned factors in a graphical form (Fig. 9.1). In the diagram, H_i represents Hypothesis i.

9.4   Research Methodology

9.4.1   Measurements

To test the hypotheses and research model, a questionnaire survey, including items for all constructs of the conceptual model, was conducted. Some of the detailed questions in the survey were modified and adapted from prior research to suit better for the context of this study. First, the detailed definitions of smart healthcare and mHealth services were given and the related items were separated in the questionnaire, so that the respondents could clearly distinguish the differences. Second, we had invited two professional doctors in a large public hospital in Hefei, China, to examine the terminology, contextual relevance, and logical consistency of the measurements. In this way, the respondents would not be confused to warrant the quality of the questionnaire. Four items were used to measure PU, three items for PEOU, three for PR, two for attitude (ATT), three for SN, three for BI; all the items in the questionnaire were measured on a 5-point Likert scale, with anchors of "strongly disagree" (1) to "strongly agree" (5). Duration of usage was employed along with frequency of use to measure the usage behavior. Formative measures were used to measure doctors' experience of using mHealth (MH). Three additional items describing different aspects of doctor's perception were measured to more completely capture the content of the doctor's experience of using mHealth. Since the respondents were Chinese doctors, the questionnaire items were translated to and administered in the Chinese language.

In order to ensure the quality and unambiguous expression of the questionnaire, a pilot test of the questionnaire was conducted prior to the release of a formal questionnaire. Forty medical students who were interested in smart healthcare services were invited to take part in the pilot and finished the questionnaire. An information systems professor was invited to modify the questionnaire according to the feedback of the pilot study. This improved veracity and feasibility before conducting the full large-scale survey.

9.4.2   Data Collection

With the permission of the hospital authorities, paper-based questionnaires were sent to five different hospitals in Anhui province between April and June 2017. These five hospitals are of three different types: two large public hospitals located in a central city, two regional hospitals located in a small city, and a local hospital in a town, respectively. The reason for selecting the five hospitals was to ensure as many types of doctors were included in our research sample as possible. A designated person in each hospital helped distribute the questionnaires to his colleagues and collect the responses back. Those who participated in the survey can get a fortune draw. A total of 534 questionnaires were returned with 50 incomplete and incorrect ones, resulting in an approximate return rate of 57.14%.

Valid responses were obtained for 484 for further data analyses, discarding 50 questionnaires with incorrect and incomplete data. There were 345 clinicians (e.g., surgery, orthopedics, gastroenterology, neurosurgery, etc.) and 139 nonclinicians (e.g., pathology, radiology, laboratory, etc.) in the sample, which permitted testing of department difference in further analyses.

9.4.3   Data Analysis and Results

Partial least squares (PLS) is a second-generation structural equation modeling (SEM) technique that is used to evaluate the causal relationship between latent constructs. The research model was tested using PLS considering its unique advantages. First, PLS makes practically no assumptions on the underlying data and does not require constructs to follow multivariate normality. Second, PLS allows latent variables to be modeled as either formative or reflective constructs with no identification problems. It can therefore be applied in a wide variety of research situations. Third, PLS is also a suitable tool to conduct multigroup analysis and test moderating effects. Both measurement model and structural model were examined in the study. We first conducted various tests to verify the reliability and validity of the measurement model for both clinical and nonclinical samples. Then, the measurement invariance of composite models (MICOM) procedure was used to further examine the measurement invariance between the two subsamples. Finally, we examined the structural model to test the proposed hypotheses by comparing the standardized path coefficient estimates between the constructs across the groups. All of these procedures are implemented in SmartPLS 3.

9.5   Measurement Model

Since the proposed conceptual model includes both reflective and formative measures, the validity of the two types of measures is evaluated.

9.5.1   Reflective Measurement Evaluation

Item reliability is assessed by evaluating the loadings of the items with their respective latent variable. Standardized loadings of the indicators should be greater than 0.7. SN2 of SN were omitted because of low factor loadings in both subsamples. As shown in Tables 9.2 and 9.3, all outer loadings of the reflective constructs ATT, BI, PEOU, PR, PU, and SN included are well above the threshold

Table 9.2 Loadings and crossloadings of clinical samples

Constructs	Items	Mean	SD	ATT	BI	PEOU	PR	PU	SN
Attitude	ATT1	3.809	0.768	**0.871**	0.451	0.436	−0.169	0.488	0.428
	ATT2	3.687	0.719	**0.832**	0.369	0.381	−0.082	0.441	0.328
BI	BI1	2.726	0.709	0.203	**0.787**	0.138	0.030	0.285	0.193
	BI2	3.986	0.832	0.524	**0.827**	0.359	−0.154	0.422	0.270
	BI3	4.162	0.778	0.466	**0.833**	0.280	−0.101	0.398	0.293
PEOU	PEOU1	3.238	1.133	0.248	0.172	**0.742**	−0.168	0.223	0.137
	PEOU2	3.600	0.740	0.444	0.292	**0.825**	−0.191	0.475	0.365
	PEOU3	3.435	0.892	0.336	0.197	**0.744**	−0.291	0.321	0.241
PR	PR1	3.290	0.896	−0.139	−0.077	−0.215	**0.723**	−0.276	−0.185
	PR2	3.096	0.981	−0.041	−0.053	−0.159	**0.716**	−0.217	−0.151
	PR3	3.301	0.994	−0.154	−0.044	−0.247	**0.728**	−0.258	−0.176
PU	PU1	4.151	0.824	0.412	0.320	0.343	−0.179	**0.789**	0.384
	PU2	3.716	0.855	0.382	0.196	0.299	−0.194	**0.709**	0.284
	PU3	3.452	0.787	0.379	0.270	0.385	−0.277	**0.707**	0.250
	PU4	4.000	0.718	0.415	0.359	0.378	−0.220	**0.774**	0.442
SN	SN1	2.783	0.807	0.365	0.362	0.305	−0.117	0.209	**0.787**
	SN2	4.058	0.767	0.425	0.383	0.348	−0.208	0.305	**0.987**

Table 9.3 Loadings and crossloadings of nonclinical samples

Constructs	Items	Mean	SD	ATT	BI	PEOU	PR	PU	SN
Attitude	ATT1	3.942	0.775	**0.916**	0.530	0.526	−0.330	0.549	0.482
	ATT2	3.770	0.816	**0.913**	0.554	0.489	−0.228	0.579	0.457
BI	BI1	2.957	0.530	0.300	**0.768**	0.238	−0.007	0.289	0.223
	BI2	4.072	0.895	0.607	**0.822**	0.355	−0.272	0.484	0.368
	BI3	3.144	0.853	0.526	**0.759**	0.229	−0.211	0.472	0.419
PEOU	PEOU1	3.273	0.750	0.239	0.139	**0.715**	0.048	0.125	0.220
	PEOU2	3.633	0.998	0.504	0.344	**0.829**	−0.229	0.454	0.359
	PEOU3	3.446	0.915	0.416	0.228	**0.756**	−0.219	0.266	0.338
PR	PR1	3.288	0.969	−0.188	−0.096	−0.179	**0.818**	−0.080	−0.158
	PR2	3.899	0.999	−0.243	−0.201	−0.032	**0.822**	−0.161	−0.161
	PR3	3.065	1.005	−0.294	−0.141	−0.316	**0.811**	−0.155	−0.246
PU	PU1	4.345	0.793	0.510	0.430	0.339	−0.119	**0.821**	0.472
	PU2	3.856	0.870	0.545	0.374	0.371	−0.189	**0.808**	0.437
	PU3	3.317	0.768	0.485	0.214	0.284	−0.176	**0.715**	0.351
	PU4	4.122	0.724	0.525	0.471	0.315	−0.063	**0.824**	0.386
SN	SN1	3.820	0.923	0.309	0.280	0.327	−0.072	0.369	**0.710**
	SN2	4.151	0.881	0.429	0.324	0.308	−0.268	0.379	**0.783**

value of 0.70 in both clinical and nonclinical samples, which suggests sufficient levels of indicator reliability. Construct reliability is assessed by Cronbach's alpha and composite reliability (CR), which should be more than 0.7. Table 9.4 shows that all the reflective constructs exceed these criteria and indicate high levels of internal consistency reliability.

Construct validity is defined by the two dimensions of convergent and discriminant validity. Convergent validity assessment is based on the average variance-extracted (AVE) values. According to Table 9.4, the results reveal that all reflectively measured constructs have AVE values of 0.529 (PU in clinical samples) or higher, which is considerably above the critical value of 0.5. Examining the cross-loadings provides initial support for the reflective constructs' discriminant validity as each reflective indicator load highest on the construct is linked to it (results refer to Tables 9.2 and 9.3). Discriminant validity is also supported when the square root of each reflective construct's AVE is larger than its correlations with other constructs. Using the item-level correlation matrix (see Table 9.4), all square roots of AVEs were significantly higher than those of the correlations in both subsamples. Another more reliable criterion to detect discriminant validity is the Heterotrait-Monotrait Ratio (HTMT). Henseler et al. [24] suggest a threshold value of 0.85 and the value of HTMT should be significantly different from 1. As can be seen from Table 9.5, all HTMT values are clearly lower than the conservative threshold value of 0.85, and the bootstrap confidence interval results of the HTMT criterion also clearly speak in favor of the discriminant validity of the constructs in both subsamples.

9.5.2   Formative Measurement Evaluation

To evaluate the formative measurement (i.e., the latent variable "MH" in our model), we followed the formative measurement model assessment procedure proposed by Hair et al. [25] Table 9.6 summarizes the results by showing the original outer weights estimates, variance inflation factor (VIF) values, t-values, p-values, and the confidence intervals derived from the percentile method. Note that the outer weight of MH1, MH4, MH5, MH6 is nonsignificant and the outer loading relatively low (i.e., <0.5); therefore, these four indicators from the model were removed from the model. The formative indicators' VIF values were all below the threshold value of 5. Therefore, it was concluded that collinearity does not reach critical levels in any of the formative constructs in both clinical and nonclinical subsamples. The outer weights of the formative indicators were analyzed for their significance and relevance by running the bootstrapping procedure. Also seen from Table 9.6, all formative indicators are significant at a 5% level. Considering all reflective and formative constructs exhibit satisfactory levels of quality in both subsamples, thus, we can proceed with the evaluation of the structural model.

Table 9.4 Results of reliability and validity analysis

Nonclinical	AVE	CR	Cronbach α	ATT	BI	PEOU	PR	PU	SN
ATT	0.726	0.841	0.724	**0.852**					
	0.836	0.911	0.804	**0.914**					
BI	0.534	0.751	0.711	0.471	**0.711**				
	0.609	0.823	0.794	0.582	**0.780**				
PEOU	0.548	0.783	0.714	0.481	0.309	**0.740**			
	0.545	0.780	0.716	0.555	0.348	**0.738**			
PR	0.682	0.864	0.783	−0.150	−0.065	−0.257	**0.826**		
	0.668	0.858	0.758	−0.306	−0.183	−0.227	**0.817**		
PU	0.529	0.817	0.711	0.546	0.401	0.486	−0.299	**0.727**	
	0.568	0.836	0.741	0.517	0.510	0.430	−0.168	**0.754**	
SN	0.602	0.774	0.722	0.445	0.387	0.360	−0.203	0.473	**0.708**
	0.547	0.707	0.711	0.503	0.410	0.427	−0.239	0.505	**0.740**

Table 9.5 HTMT of clinical and nonclinical samples

	ATT	BI	PEOU	PR	PU	SN
ATT	0					
	0					
BI	0.706	0				
	0.812	0				
PEOU	0.745	0.567	0			
	0.729	0.477	0			
PR	0.220	0.206	0.369	0		
	0.377	0.293	0.382	0		
PU	0.825	0.714	0.696	0.404	0	
	0.763	0.715	0.563	0.247	0	
SN	0.542	0.365	0.540	0.741	0.315	0
	0.331	0.222	0.225	0.730	0.348	0

Table 9.6 Bootstrapping results for formative constructs

Formative constructs (mHealth)	Formative indicators	Outer loadings	VIF	t	p	95% CI	$p < 0.05$?
Clinical	MH2	0.508 (0.970)	2.582	4.346	0.0000	[0.277, 0.742]	Yes
	MH3	0.522 (0.971)	2.510	4.463	0.0000	[0.278, 0.743]	Yes
Nonclinical	MH2	0.695 (0.978)	2.792	3.387	0.0005	[0.262, 1.085]	Yes
	MH3	0.552 (0.909)	2.792	3.558	0.0007	[0.112, 0.774]	Yes

9.5.3 Measurement Invariance Assessment

The MICOM procedure [23] was used to test measurement invariance before testing differences in structural paths across the clinical and nonclinical groups. The procedure consists of three steps assessing (1) configural invariance, (2) compositional invariance and (3) equal mean values and variances. To compare the standardized path coefficients across groups at least configural and compositional invariance has to be established. Running MICOM in SmartPLS 3 usually automatically establishes configural invariance. Compositional invariance means that the indicator weights being used to calculate the composite's scores remain the same. There is compositional invariance if the correlation between the calculated scores of the two groups does not differ significantly, e.g., c equals one. A permutation test reveals if correlation c is significantly different from one or not. According to the MICOM results in Table 9.7, PR has the lowest c value with 0.989, which is very close to one. Overall, compositional invariance is supported for all composites with the correlations lying within the 95% confidence interval of the distribution of the correlation testing 5000 permutations. Finally, we assess the composites' equality of mean

Table 9.7 MICOM results

Composite	c-Value	95% CI	Compositional invariance?
ATT	0.999	0.996	Yes
BI	0.991	0.979	Yes
PEOU	0.999	0.976	Yes
PR	0.989	0.917	Yes
PU	0.998	0.993	Yes
SN	0.994	0.954	Yes
MH	0.995	0.974	Yes
	Diff mean		Equal means?
ATT	−0.164	[−0.201, 0.200]	Yes
BI	−0.110	[−0.197, 0.198]	Yes
PEOU	−0.041	[−0.203, 0.193]	Yes
PR	0.147	[−0.197, −.196]	Yes
PU	−0.238	[−0.196, 0.199]	No
SN	−0.101	[−0.198, 0.201]	Yes
MH	−0.090	[−0.191, 0.203]	Yes
			Equal variance?
ATT	−0.272	[−0.249, 0.269]	No
BI	−0.132	[−0.267, 0.291]	Yes
PEOU	−0.025	[−0.261, 0.284]	Yes
PR	−0.004	[−0.283, 0.320]	Yes
PU	−0.099	[−0.226, 0.249]	Yes
SN	−0.428	[−0.381, 0.456]	No
MH	0.160	[−0.275, 0.322]	Yes

values and variances across clinical and nonclinical subgroups. However, the mean value of PU and the variances of ATT and SN showed significant differences across the two groups. Thus, partial measurement invariance had been established implying the need for "meaningful multigroup analyses by comparing the standardized coefficients in the structural model."

9.5.4 Hypotheses Testing and Multigroup Analysis

To ensure the stability of the model developed for testing the research hypotheses, the PLS bootstrap resampling procedure was used with an iteration of 5000 subsamples drawn with replacement from the initial sample. Figure 9.2 presents the estimated results of the structural model of both clinical and nonclinical samples. Table 9.8 provides the significance testing results of the path coefficient estimates.

For both clinical and nonclinical samples, hypotheses 1, 2, 3, 4, and 5 dealt with relationships of the TAM model and are supported and significant with $p < 0.05$. In both groups, the relationships between PU and ATT (H3) as well as PEOU and PU

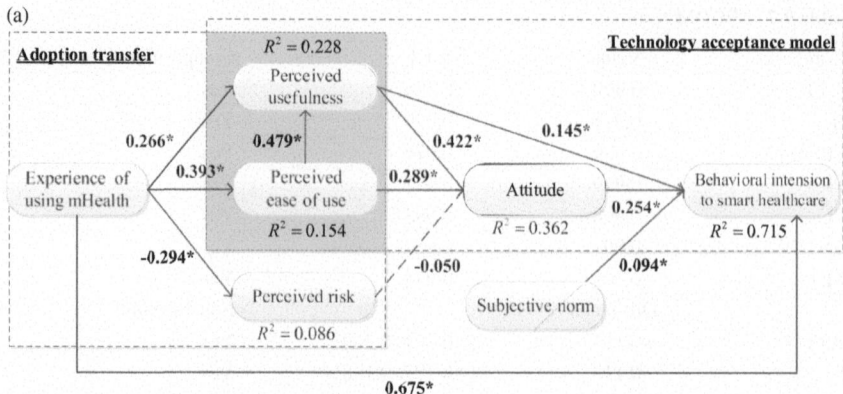

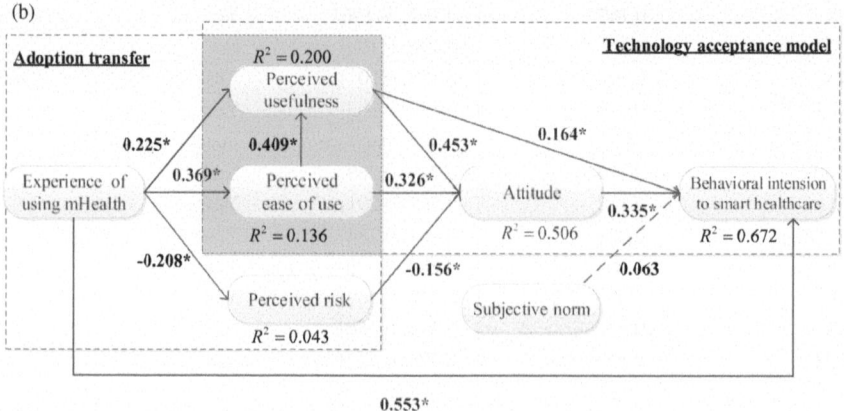

Fig. 9.2 Estimation of structural model for different departments. (**a**) Clinical department and (**b**) nonclinical department. Note: Significant paths shown in solid line. R^2: coefficient of determination, *$p < 0.05$

(H5) are significant, each demonstrating a medium effect size ($f2$) larger than 0.15 [26]. The effect of ATT on BI (H1) as well as PEOU on ATT (H4) is significant in both samples, with effect size displaying a stronger effect in the nonclinical sample. Inconsistent with our hypotheses (H6 and H7), the path between SN and BI is only significant for the clinical sample ($\beta = 0.094$, $t = 2.394$, $p = 0.016$), while the path between PR and ATT is only significant in the negative direction for the nonclinical sample ($\beta = -0.156$, $t = 2.744$, $p = 0.006$).

For the constructs of technology transfer, PLS results show that MH positively influences PU and PEOU, while it negatively influences PR in both subsamples. Thus, hypotheses 8, 9, and10 are all supported. Furthermore, as predicted, the high path coefficients in both groups show that there is indeed a direct relationship between the experience of using mHealth and doctors' BI on smart healthcare services. Hence, hypothesis 11 is supported. In particular, in both samples, the

Table 9.8 Differences in path estimators between the two subsamples

Hypothesis	Relationship	Support?	Clinical $f2$	Nonclinical $f2$	Clinical p	Nonclinical p	Difference	Sig?
H1	ATT → BI	Yes	0.145	0.194	0.000	0.000	−0.084	No
H2	PU → BI	Yes	0.047	0.046	0.000	0.029	−0.019	No
H3	PU → ATT	Yes	0.203	0.333	0.000	0.000	−0.030	No
H4	PEOU→ATT	Yes	0.099	0.170	0.000	0.000	−0.036	No
H5	PEOU→PU	Yes	0.300	0.203	0.000	0.000	0.071	No
H6	SN → BI	1Yes 2No	0.022	0.008	0.016	0.293	0.031	At 0.05
H7	PR → ATT	1No 2Yes	0.004	0.047	0.000	0.006	0.206	At 0.05
H8	MH → PU	Yes	0.106	0.119	0.000	0.007	−0.059	No
H9	MH → PEOU	Yes	0.209	0.200	0.000	0.000	−0.077	No
H10	MH → PR	Yes	0.109	0.101	0.000	0.024	0.086	No
H11	MH → BI	Yes	1.545	0.881	0.000	0.000	0.123	At 0.05

experience of using mHealth displays a medium effect on PEOU ($f2 > 0.15$) and the strongest positive effect on BI ($f2 > 0.35$).

The predictive power of the proposed structural model can be described as moderate since the R^2 values of BI construct are higher than 0.50 in both samples (see Fig. 9.2). The R^2 values of PU, PEOU, and PR are weak for both samples. In contrast, the R^2 value of ATT is significantly higher in the nonclinical sample. Overall, even if most of the hypotheses are supported across the two groups, there are also some significant differences, partly confirming H12.

9.6 Discussion and Implications

This study sought to explain doctors' adoption intention of smart healthcare services from a technology transfer perspective. As shown in Fig. 9.2, the experiments present some key insights to address the questions. First, the current model explains 71.5% and 67.2% of the variance in doctors' intention to use smart healthcare services in clinical and nonclinical department, respectively, which indicates a relatively high explanatory power. The relationships among physicians' BI, attitude, PU, and PEOU are all significant in both subgroups. PU is the most strong and significant determinant of attitude on smart healthcare services for both clinicians and nonclinicians.

Second, the results of multigroup analysis demonstrate that in nonclinical department, SN is not significant in determining BI (H6) while PR is significant in determining attitude (H7). These conclusions are exactly the opposite for clinicians. The possible reasons for this might be related to the occupational characteristics of nonclinicians. First, nonclinicians in this study mainly include pathologists and radiologists. In China, physicians of these specialties are relatively scarce, especially those with experienced domain knowledge and exquisite skills. Therefore, unlike clinicians, perceived social pressure from superiors or colleagues is relatively smaller in nonclinicians. The application of smart healthcare is better and more mature in the field of department of dermatology, pathology, and imaging. With the rapid development of smart healthcare services, some concerns have recently surfaced that nonclinicians' authority would be challenged by these new intelligent products and even be replaced by those products [27]. Therefore, PR is found to be strongly negative associated with nonclinicians' attitudes.

Third, TAM was extended by including an external factor, experience of using mHealth, as the antecedent of the TAM constructs. Results clearly show that in both subgroups, the experience of using mHealth positively affects PU and PEOU, while negatively affects PR. Moreover, as the results indicate, doctors' experience of using mHealth shows a significant direct impact on their BI on smart healthcare services in both clinical and nonclinical departments. That is, doctors' technology transfer behavior probably exists between mHealth and smart healthcare services. More importantly, the experience of using mHealth is the most important determinant of BI on smart healthcare services for both clinicians and nonclinicians and the relationship is more significant in the clinical department. These findings are consistent with our hypothesis of the moderating effect of department difference (i.e., H12).

9.6.1 Theoretical Implications

From a theoretical point of view, the contribution of this study to IT acceptance research is multifold. First and foremost, this study is among the pioneering studies focusing on doctors' adoption intention of the AI-driven smart healthcare services. This study adds to the current knowledge in the fields of technology acceptance and healthcare IT implementation. More relevant research on adoption intention and usage behavior toward smart healthcare services is worth making.

Another major theoretical contribution of the present study is including the experience of using mHealth as an antecedent to understand its relationship with doctors' BI on smart healthcare services. This study explores doctors' perceptions and BIs between different IT products from a technology transfer perspective. Although overlooked in previous studies, relationships among nonsubstitute IT products have been found to be significant in this study. These findings may provide a novel perspective for future research.

Furthermore, this study also provides some evidence on the need to incorporate other moderate variables to increase the explanatory value of theoretical models. That is, department difference should not be overlooked and discarded from acceptance models in the context of healthcare.

9.7 Conclusion

This study found two important points:

First, healthcare services marketers and salesmen should pay more attention to doctors with mHealth using experience. They could work to establish stronger links with doctors using mHealth to expand the market for smart healthcare by market segmentation. For instance, larger hospitals such as medical centers possess the necessary resources and skills to integrate the innovation with medical personnel efficiently and effectively, and the coverage of mHealth is undoubted larger. Healthcare services marketers and salesmen could turn this into an advantage, in order to achieve wider acceptance and more frequent use of smart healthcare services.

Second, it is necessary to focus on the key factors that influence adoption intention of smart healthcare services and develop different marketing strategies for doctors in different departments, with the ultimate goal of expanding the market and attracting potential users. For example, both clinicians and nonclinicians tend to go for useful and easy-to-use smart healthcare services, while PR is more significant for nonclinicians. Thus, to effectively encourage doctors to use smart healthcare, the products designed should be convenient and useful and developers must think of how to eliminate nonclinicians' feelings of disruption about smart healthcare services for their existing work practices.

References

1. Davis, F. (1989). Perceived usefulness, perceived ease of use, and user acceptance of information technology. *MIS Quarterly, 13*(3), 319–339.
2. Hsieh, P.-J. (2015). Physicians' acceptance of electronic medical records exchange: An extension of the decomposed TPB model with institutional trust and perceived risk. *International Journal of Medical Informatics, 84*(1), 1–14.
3. Khor, K. S., & Hazen, B. T. (2017). Remanufactured products purchase intentions and behavior: Evidence from Malaysia. *International Journal of Production Research, 55*(8), 2149–2162.
4. Ahnadi, H., Nilashi, M., Shahmoradi, L., & Ibrahim, O. (2017). Hospital information system adoption: Expert perspectives on an adoption framework for Malaysian public hospitals. *Computers in Human Behavior, 67*, 161–189.
5. Beglaryan, M., Petrosyan, V., & Bunker, E. (2017). Development of a tripolar model of technology acceptance: Hospital-based physicians' perspective on HER. *International Journal of Medical Informatics, 102*, 50–61.
6. Brown, W., Yen, P. Y., Rojas, M., & Schnall, R. (2013). Assessment of the health IT usability evaluation model (health-ITUEM) for evaluating mobile health (mHealth) technology. *Journal of Biomedical Informatics, 46*(6), 1080–1087.
7. Lee, W., Xiong, L., & Hu, C. (2012). The effect of Facebook users' arousal and valence on intention to go to the festival: Applying an extension of the technology acceptance model. *International Journal of Hospitality Management, 31*(3), 819–827.
8. Maio, R., Ru, Q., Wang, Z., Song, Y., Zhang, H., Sun, Q., & Jiang, Z. (2017). Factors that influence users' adoption intention of mobile health: A structural equation modeling approach. *International Journal of Production Research, 55*(19), 5801–5815.
9. Venkatesh, V., & Davis, F. (1996). A model of the antecedents of perceived ease of use: Development and test. *Decision Sciences, 27*(3), 451–481.
10. Dishaw, M. T., & Strong, D. M. (1999). Extending the technology acceptance model with task-technology fit constructs. *Information and Management, 36*(1), 9–21.
11. Morris, M. G., Hall, M., Davis, G. B., Davis, F. D., & Walton, S. M. (2003). User acceptance of information technology: Toward a unified view. *MIS Quarterly, 27*(3), 425–478.
12. Riemenschneider, C. K., Harrison, D. A., & Mykytyn, P. P. (2003). Understanding IT adoption decisions in small business: Integrating current theories. *Information and Management, 40*(4), 269–285.
13. Bauer, R. A. (1967). Consumer behavior as risk taking? In *Risk taking and information handling in consumer behavior* (pp. 23–33). Boston: Graduate School of Business Administration, Harvard University.
14. Koudstaal, M., Sloof, R., & van Praag, M. (2016). Risk, undertainty, and entrepreneurship: Evidence from a lab-in-the-field experiment. *Management Science, 62*(10), 2897–2915.
15. Tandon, U., Kiran, R., & Sah, A. N. (2016). Understanding online shopping adoption in India: Unified theory of acceptance and use of technology 2 (UTAUT2) with perceived risk application. *Service Science, 8*(4), 420–437.

16. Weiss, L., & Johar, G. V. (2013). Egocentric categorization and product judgment: Seeing your traits in what you own (and their opposite in what you don't). *Journal of Consumer Research, 40*(1), 185–201.
17. Istepanian, R. S. H., & Al-Anzi, T. (2018). M-health 2.0: New perspectives on mobile health, machine learning and big data analytics. *Methods.* https://doi.org/10.1016/j.ymeth.2018.05.015.
18. Moores, T. T. (2012). Towards an integrated model of IT acceptance in healthcare. *Decision Support Systems, 53*(3), 507–516.
19. Zhang, W.-G., Zhang, Q., Mizgier, K. J., & Zhang, Y. (2017). Integrating the customers' perceived risks and benefits into the triple-channel retailing. *International Journal of Medical Informatics, 108*, 97–109.
20. Chang, I.-C., & Hsu, H.-M. (2012). Predicting medical staff intention to use an online reporting system with modified unified theory of acceptance and use of technology. *Telemedicine and E-Health, 18*(1), 67–73.
21. Kingston, M. J., Evans, S. M., Smith, B. J., & Berry, J. G. (2004). Attitudes of doctors and nurses towards incident reporting: A qualitative analysis. *The Medical Journal of Australia, 181*, 36–39.
22. Gagnon, M. P., Ghandour, E. K., Kengne Talla, P., Dimonyan, D., Godin, G., Labrecque, M., Ouimet, M., & Rousseau, M. (2014). Electronic health record acceptance by physicians: Testing an integrated theoretical model. *Journal of Biomedical Informatics, 48*, 17–27.
23. Rosenkrantz, A. B., Sherwin, J., Prithiani, C. P., Ostrow, D., & Recht, M. P. (2016). Technology-assisted virtual consultation for medical imaging. *Journal of the American College of Radiology, 13*(8), 995–1002.
24. Henseler, J., Ringle, C. M., & Sarstedt, M. (2016). Testing measurement invariance of composites using partial least squares. *International Marketing Review, 33*(3), 405–431.
25. Hair, J. F., Thomas, G., Hult, M., Ringle, C. M., & Sarstedt, M. (2017). *A primer on partial least squares structural equation modeling (PLS-SEM)* (2nd ed.). Thousand Oaks, CA: Sage.
26. Cohen, J. (1977). Chi-square tests for goodness of fit and contingency tables. In *Statistical power analysis for the behavioral sciences* (2nd ed., pp. 215–271). New York: Academic Press.
27. Esteva, A., Kuprel, B., Novoa, R. A., Ko, J., Swetter, S. M., Blau, H. M., & Thrun, S. (2017). Dermatologist-level classification of skin cancer with deep neural networks. *Nature, 542*(7639), 115–118.

Chapter 10
Healthcare Efficiency Modeling

Abstract Pandemic planning depends a great deal on hospital capacity. COVID-19 created great strain on hospital bed resources in Wuhan, Milan, New York City, and elsewhere. Hospitals today need to provide basic services to satisfy community demands, and at the same time offer specialization, to enhance their competitiveness. From a management perspective, measuring and ranking the hospital's efficiency appropriately is complex because their funding is affected by many factors. This chapter presents a DEA model to assess capacity to accept new patients considering resource costs.

Modern health systems face challenges calling for efficiency. Data envelopment analysis (DEA) offers a means to measure their performance. This chapter presents a DEA analysis ranking 329 hospitals in the US public healthcare sector. Performance dimensions cover cost and revenue, treatment environment and capacity, labors, and technical quality. Although DEA is a systemic approach, the associated score rankings appear to be inconsistent with respect to the small changes in parameters. Wu and Wu developed a robust DEA approach that takes account of the uncertainty of outputs and solution complexity. Ranking results show that efficient nonprofit hospitals are more sensitive to the development of technical innovation, while the performances of efficient profit-driven hospitals are more affected by the reduction of patient numbers. We also find that the robust approach presented here decreases risk-to-mean ratios by 7% for the profit-driven hospital group.

Systematic approaches have been applied to identify high performers and important factors in the hospital sector. One popular assessment strategy is to rank aggregative output to input ratios that represent the organization productiveness. DEA pursues the optimal ratios to rank the relative position of specific units relative to the peers.

This chapter draws heavily from Wu and Wu (2019), Risk-based robust evaluation of hospital efficiency, IEEE Systems Journal 13(2), 1906–1914, with permission

Ranking risk can change DEA assessment due to changing of inputs or outputs of the system under different future scenarios. For example, the combination of recent reforms in the US healthcare system that extend insurance coverage and big data innovation in healthcare substantially change health system structure and lead to different patient visit patterns. An example pointed out by the Centers for Medicare and Medicaid Services is the use of quality indicators to improve the hospital service through measurement of performance [1]. However, some of indices, such as technology, are ambiguous or difficult to change over long periods and have less bearing on evaluation systems. These dynamic factors should be taken into account when applying DEA-based models.

Wu and Wu evaluated hospital risk efficiency considering measures of quality of performance and compare results to those of the standard DEA model to illustrate the advantages of the proposed approach. Specifically, we developed a robust DEA counterpart to prevent the impact of the perturbations from output observations. We show that hospitals that pursue profit most can obtain better rankings when faced with changes in patient load, while nonprofit hospitals benefit more from using technical innovation to improve their efficiency. Even in inefficient hospitals, the robust approach generally obtains an average 7% performance improvement in terms of risk-to-mean ratios.

10.1   Nominal and Robust DEA Models

There are a number of basic DEA models:

10.1.1   Basic CCR Model

The first is named after Charnes, Cooper, and Rhodes. Assuming that there are n Decision Making Units (DMUs) to be evaluated, which are represented by $j = 1$, ..., n, respectively. Each DMU has m different inputs and obtains s different outputs. The input and output vectors of DMU_j are $X_j = (x_{1j}, x_{2j}, \ldots, x_{mj})^T > 0$ and $Y_j = (y_{1j}, y_{2j}, \ldots, y_{sj})^T > 0 (j = 1, \ldots, n)$. For DMU_j, its DEA efficiency value can be defined by:

$$E_j = \frac{\sum_{k=1}^{s} u_k y_{kj}}{\sum_{i=1}^{m} v_i x_{ij}} = \frac{U^T Y_j}{V^T X_j}, j = 1, \ldots, n,$$

where $V = (v_1, v_2, \ldots, v_m)^T$ and $U = (u_1, u_2, \ldots, u_s)^T$ are the weights of the input and output vectors, respectively.

For $p = 1, \ldots, n$, the CCR model can be expressed by the following formula:

$$\max \frac{U^T Y_p}{V^T X_p}, \tag{10.1}$$

$$\text{s.t.} \quad \frac{U^T Y_j}{V^T X_j} \leq 1, \quad j = 1, \ldots, n, \tag{10.2}$$

$$U \geq 0, V \geq 0. \tag{10.3}$$

Since the CCR output angle assumes that for all DMUs, the amount of input factors is constant, it can be equivalent to the following easy-to-solve linear programming form:

$$\max U^T Y_p, \tag{10.4}$$

$$\text{s.t.} V^T X_p = 1, \tag{10.5}$$

$$\frac{U^T Y_j}{V^T X_j} \leq 1, j = 1, \ldots, n, \tag{10.6}$$

$$U \geq 0, V \geq 0. \tag{10.7}$$

Models (10.4), (10.5), (10.6) and (10.7) can be efficiently solved by methods such as the interior point algorithm, which is tractable for practical sized problems. After solving models (10.4), (10.5), (10.6) and (10.7), a score E_j is calculated. If $E_j = 1$, then the jth DMU is efficient and dominations DMUs that don't have $E_j = 1$. If $E_j < 1$, we can infer that the jth DMU is not efficient and adjustment of its inputs and/or outputs to improve its E_j to be rated efficient. We can control inputs, but outputs usually are uncertain which can significantly affect the CCR efficient score values. This disadvantage motivated us to develop a relative robust model.

10.1.2 Robust DEA Model

Robust optimization is a popular method to cope with uncertainty and has been widely accepted by academia and industry because of its theoretical and computational advantages. In this section, we show a robust optimization approach to immunize with the change of coefficient of output. Setting that the coefficients of output y in (P_1) can violate $\tilde{y}$ from the observation, for example, $\bar{y}_{rj}$ are the observations of output data, $\tilde{y}_{rj}$ are the added variables which means the perturbation of the output, and $\tilde{y}_{rj}$ followed a distribution associated with dimension r. Then we can describe for any DMU lie in an ellipsoid ε_j with a center $\bar{y}_j$ and $P_j \in R^{s \times s}$, $\varsigma_j \in R^{s \times 1}$, then

$$\bar{y}_j + \tilde{y}_j \in \varepsilon_j = \{\bar{y}_j + P_j\varsigma_j | \|\varsigma_j\| \le 1\}.$$

Any vector u_j can be mapped into the ellipsoid ε_j by the relation:

$$\varsigma_j = \frac{P_j^T U}{\|P_j^T U\|_2},$$

where P_j is the standard deviation matrix and ς_j is the length of vector of output data. For the objective function of CCR:

$$\max_{u_p \in R^s} \inf_{\bar{y}_p + \tilde{y}_p \in \varepsilon_p} \left\{ \sum_{r=1}^{s} u_r \left(\bar{y}_{rp} + \tilde{y}_{rp} \right) \right\} = \max_{u_p \in R^s} \left\{ \inf_{\|\varsigma_p\| \le 1} \left(\sum_{r=1}^{s} u_r \bar{y}_{rp} + \varsigma_p^T P_p^T U \right) \right\}$$

$$= \max_{u_p \in R^s} \left\{ \sum_{r=1}^{s} u_r \bar{y}_{rp} - \frac{U^T P_p P_p^T U}{\|P_p^T U\|_2} \right\}$$

$$= \max_{u_p \in R^s} \left\{ \sum_{r=1}^{s} u_r \bar{y}_{rp} - \frac{\|P_p^T U\|_2^2}{\|P_p^T U\|_2} \right\}$$

$$= \max_{u_p \in R^s} \left\{ \sum_{r=1}^{s} u_r \bar{y}_{rp} - \|P_p^T U\|_2 \right\}.$$

For the constraint [2] of CCR:

$$\text{Sup}_{\tilde{y}_j} \left\{ \sum_{r=1}^{s} u_{rj} \left(\bar{y}_{rj} + \tilde{y}_{rj} \right) | \bar{y}_{rj} + \tilde{y}_{rj} \in \varepsilon_j \right\} = \text{Sup}_{\|\varsigma_j\| \le 1} \sum_{r=1}^{s} u_{rj} \bar{y}_{rj} + \varsigma_j^T P_j^T U$$

$$= \sum_{r=1}^{s} u_{rj} \bar{y}_{rj} + \|P_j^T U\|_2.$$

Then the following (P_2) are obtained:

$$Min - t, \tag{10.8}$$

Subject to

$$-\sum_{r=1}^{s} u_r \bar{y}_{rp} + \|P_p^T U\|_2 \le -t, \tag{10.9}$$

$$\sum_{i=1}^{m} v_i \bar{x}_{ip} = 1, \qquad (10.10)$$

$$-\sum_{i=1}^{m} v_i \bar{x}_{ij} + \sum_{r=1}^{s} u_r \bar{y}_{rj} + \left\| P_j^T U \right\|_2 \leq 0, \forall j = 1, \ldots, n, \qquad (10.11)$$

$$v_i, u_r \geq 0. \qquad (10.12)$$

Models (10.8), (10.9), (10.10), (10.11) and (10.12) is a second-order cone programming (SOCP) formulation which can also be solved efficiently like its nominal counterpart. Specifically, this problem was handled using SeDuMi [2] which is a free special-purpose code for second-order cone programming based on interior point algorithm.

The proposed models (10.8), (10.9), (10.10), (10.11) and (10.12) considered both correlated and uncorrelated relations between the outputs along different dimensions through the norm restrictions in the evaluation system. The correlations between the factors also play important roles to determine the ranking position in reality and should be considered by the decision-makers. Therefore, we believe that our robust DEA model is generally enough to extend to other DEA-based models, and our accompanied robust analysis in Section IV can be seen as one example for many other robust DEA assessment applications.

10.2 Efficiency Analysis for US Hospitals

10.2.1 Data

Wu and Wu collected hospital data from the New York Statewide Planning and Research Cooperative System (SPARCS), who is one of the major agencies to help hospitals and healthcare organizations to optimize their financial planning and monitor surgery services for inpatients, and provides necessary data for this research. The dataset contained data on 355 governmental and nongovernmental hospitals in the United States in 2016. After deleting observations with missing data, 329 hospitals containing all inputs and outputs used in the DEA models were available. Of these, 34 were teaching hospitals mainly located in urban (33) area and 295 were nonteaching hospitals distributed in rural (52) and urban (243), respectively. 6 inputs and 5 outputs that are used for score calculation from the models are described in Table 10.1.

The percentage of private rooms had both positive and negative impact on hospital performance. Private rooms increased the chance of curability, but may also cost more resources and limited hospital capacity to accept new patients. Setting

Table 10.1 Input and output descriptions

Parameters	Metrics	Description
Input 1	Relative private room ratio	Measure treatment satisfaction
Input 2	Number of licensed beds	Capacity of inpatient treatment
Input 3	Nurse FTEs per bed	Workload hours per bed converted to nurses required
Input 4	Payroll expense	Cost of labor force
Input 5	Supply expense	Cost affecting hospital performance
Input 6	Relative physical space per bed	Satisfy standard level
Output 1	Specialization index	Reduce cost, enhance service quality (efficiency)
Output 2	Technology index	Technology-driven hospitals have a better reputation
Output 3	Emergency visits	Key hospital service metric
Output 4	Total outpatient visits	Key quality metric
Output 5	Inpatient discharges	DRG-weighted inpatient discharges in terms of the overall payment

Table 10.2 Average physical space per bed requirement in SF

Beds	100–199	200–299	300–399	400–499	$\geq$500
Average space per bed (SF)	9.8	10.1	9	8	9.4

a single-room rate can satisfy all parties and enhance hospital effectiveness. A reasonable private-room rate, $\alpha_1 = 50\%$, is used to construct Input 1 in our study. The number of certified beds (Input 2) is an important factor that affects financial performance among most of the private hospitals. Input 3 denotes how many nurses are required to complete the workload hours per bed in daily operation. From hospital managers' perspective, a smaller value means more efficiency of the nurse labor, and potentially more patients can be served. Inputs 4 and 5 directly measure the financial aspect in hospital efficiency. Intuitively, the smaller the better. We adjust the total physical space according to the number of beds a hospital own. Plenty of space per bed improves patient satisfaction. However, it also decreases the number of beds and may affect the total number of patients. Input 6 ensures the physical space per bed is close to the average level, α_2, displayed in Table 10.2.

For example, if one hospital has 250 beds with 3500 sqft available, and the expected bed space equals 10.1, then associated input 6 is calculated by $\left|\frac{3500}{250} - 10.1\right| = 3.9$. Overall, the inputs represent the performance metrics include cost (Inputs 4 and 5), treatment environment (Inputs 1, 2, and 6), and labor efficiency (Input 3).

The outputs, on the other side, focus on the performance include the ability to receive patients (Outputs 3 and 4), innovation (Outputs 1 and 2), and financial efficiency (Output 5). The hospitals improve their services as a result of substantial reforms in technical innovations. First, the index of specialization (IoS) characterizes and integrates the information difference between a hospital's product or service lines and the baseline proportion of associated categories. Mathematically,

$$IoS_k = \sum_{i=1}^{I} p_{ik} \, ln\left(\frac{p_{ik}}{\phi_i}\right),$$

where p_{ik} is the proportion of cases in the kth hospital observed in category i, and ϕ_i denotes the baseline proportion of cases in the same category i. The index equals zero when all service categories are the same as the baseline categories, i.e. $p_i = \phi_i$, and it increases as case-mix fractions diverge, which means the hospital limits the array of services it provides. Empirical evidence shows that the high level of hospital specialization, represented by Output 1, can enhance the competitiveness by utilizing the resources more efficiently and reduce the cost significantly. The higher value of the index reflects more competitive advantage the hospital obtained. Thus, the index is included in our analysis.

Technology development plays an important role in treating incurable diseases. The hospital technology index measures the capital-intensive medical technology based on three relevant factors, i.e. core technology, highly specialized technology, and therapeutic cancer technology. Each factor includes subitems that represent standard hospital therapeutic and diagnostic procedures, and the reliability and validity of the treatment across different hospitals can be tracked and compared. The construction process is descried as follows. Each subitem is first assigned a loading according to the performance, and then the weighted item is transformed to Z score. Finally, the three subscales are aggregated into an index score. The advantage of a composite index lies in its greater reliability and allows taking account of large data sets. Therefore, Output 2 is one of the considerations in the modern healthcare system. Outputs 3 and 4 are typical indicators that reflect the service abilities of different departments in a hospital. Finally, since DRG-weighted inpatient discharges comprised a large portion of hospital incomes, we adopt Output 5 as a representative of the financial effectiveness.

There is a tremendous difference between our results and the existing work in terms of categorizing and risk analysis of hospital performance. First, unlike the grouping of hospitals as either congested or non-congested in Clement et al. [3] Wu and Wu distinguished the samples across profit and nonprofit criteria, which ranks the hospitals from a totally different perspective. Second, Ozcan [4] focused on sensitivity analysis on the input side, but Wu and Wu examined hospital performance by adjusting the parameter based on prior information of outputs. Previous work showed that relevant technologies can affect hospital performance significantly [1]. In the same manner, Wu and Wu investigated the impact of technology but more focused on the stability of the ranking.

The hospitals were grouped by profit level and listed the statistics of inputs and outputs in Table 10.3.

Hospitals were arranged in ascending order according to profit-seeking. Group 1 consisted of 132 nonprofit hospitals, while the 31 hospitals in Group 3 sought to

Table 10.3 Input and output statistics

	Range group 1 (132)	Mean	Range group 2 (166)	Mean	Range group 3 (31)	Mean
Input 1	[1, 2500]	1118	[4, 2500]	1543	[144, 2500]	1553
Input 2	[19, 1119]	292.88	[4, 1894]	202.43	[0, 968]	257.65
Input 3	[0.16, 3.35]	1.32	[0, 9.67]	1.47	[0, 5.11]	1.47
Input 4	[1.65, 51.5] M	7.88	[2.8, 39] M	3.9	[6.1, 164.2] M	14.09
Input 5	[2.78, 75.7] M	11.04	[3.7, 51.1] M	5.11	[1.02, 126.3] M	14.13
Input 6	[0.12, 126.4]	14.3	[0.07, 1021]	44.3	[0.26, 141.9]	32
Output 1	[8.45, 61.48]	12.7	[5.36, 94.96]	27.85	[8.13, 49.25]	13.66
Output 2	[0, 8]	4.95	[0, 8]	3.55	[1, 8] K	4.52
Output 3	[0, 163.6] K	45.4	[0, 273.8] K	25.5	[0, 173.7] K	39.5
Output 4	[0, 1387] K	143.4	[0, 436.4] K	55.1	[0, 2211.1]	352.4
Output 5	[302, 75,206]	13,766	[102, 60,864]	7543	[577, 62,769]	13,074

Note: Inputs 3 and 4 measured by million per year; Outputs 3, 4, and 5 measured by thousand per unit

maximize financial returns. The other 166 hospitals were between these two groups and set a lower profit target. As can be seen, 298 out of 329 (90.58%) hospitals took social responsibility into account. The minimal value of Input 1 in group 3 is 144, much larger than those from other groups. This can be explained by the fact that the hospitals in group 3 generally are willing to increase the number of single rooms to earn more profits, but this also deviates from the setting ratio and lead to undesirable larger distance (1118 vs. 1553 on average). The maximum number of licensed beds (Input 2) in group 3 is smaller than in other groups, and the corresponding range is narrower compared with other ranges. This is reasonable because profit-priority hospitals tend to control the available resource like beds number to enhance the marginal profit. This indicator also offers a benchmark to other groups in the evaluation system.

It is surprising to see that for Input 3, Nurse FTEs per bed, the nonprofit hospitals in group 1 performed better than profit-derived hospitals from other groups (see the average values of 1.32 vs. 1.47) or range concentrations. This comparison indicates that more workload per bed is required for the nurses in profit-seeking hospitals, which subsequently increases revenue for selling additional services. On the other hand, nonprofit hospitals may only supply the basic treatment for patients and lead to small values of Input 3 because of the reduction of total work hours. Group 3 has highest payroll expense (Input 4) and supply expense (Input 5) on average, but also the largest Std/Mean ratios (2.23 and 1.83, respectively) among the entire data set.

The ratio of the standard deviation to the mean measures relative variability of its sample average. The ratio involves two components where the first one is the uncertainty of the ratio due to limited observations, and the second one is the potential damage to the performance for a specific hospital under the ranking system. Our consideration can be seen as one application of the risk definition in Kaplan and Garrick [5] who explained risk as an aggregation of the uncertainty and some possible loss or damage that might be received in future. The ratio values represent high operational uncertainties under a competitive environment. Based on the ranking results, the inefficient hospital may lose or receive less funding support, and this loss can cause real harm to the hospital in the long run. However, the worse score may be resulted by the perturbation of the indicators rather than the real changing of the performance, and our work tries to reduce the impact of improper ranking. The hospitals in group 1 have relatively smaller and stable expenses due to the nonprofit feature. Input 6 integrates the effect of different resources, and we see that group 1 has the best position close to the expected values in Table II. An interesting observation is that group 2 has the worst Std/Mean ratio (2.69) with a mean value of 44.3 and standard deviation 119.4, mainly because there is ample physical bed space in these hospitals.

Regarding Output 1, the average specialization index of group 2 is higher than the values of other groups, see both means and standard deviations. This denotes that the middle groups are more likely to use specialized services for their patients. Additionally, all these groups have a similar level of technology index, represented by Output 2, which means they all realize the importance of the technology innovation. Another key performance of a hospital is the number of emergency and outpatient patient visits. It is interesting to see that nonprofit hospitals have relatively larger and stable emergency visits (Output 3) compared with values from pure profit-derived hospitals (45.4 > 39.5). In contrast, group 3 has a better performance in terms of total outpatient visits (352.4 > 143.4 on Output 4). Patient visits by hospitals in group 2 were, as shown by larger Std/Mean ratios. These observations tell us that hospitals in groups 1 and 3 play different roles for accepting patients, and they complement each other. Finally, Output 5 indicates that inpatient discharges between groups 1 and 3 are close, partially because profit-derived hospitals focus on the high service quality and accept less number of inpatients. It is clear to see that group 2 generates the least revenue on average due to a limited number of inpatients.

As shown above, one major issue of using the classic CCR model to evaluate hospital efficiency lies in unreliable outputs. For example, emergency visits (Output 3) may be hard to predict and be affected by many factors such as population changes or different lengths of stay of patients. If the emergency visits of evaluated DMU dropped 35% and other hospitals' parameters remained same, we found that 21 out of 75 (28%) efficiency DMU became inefficient under the new score system, and the score of worst instance jumped to 0.7573 from original efficient score 1. In addition, the number of efficient DMU across groups changed from [34, 34, 7] by original DEA system to [25, 23, 6], which denotes that large portion of efficient hospitals in groups 1 and 2 will be impacted by the perturbation of emergency visits significantly.

Traditional sensitivity analysis for nominal model cannot control uncertainty actively. It just offers a possible solution change under each scenario in terms of the changing of the model parameter. Through adjusting the radius of the ellipsoid for each uncertain output, the robust counterpart takes account all possible combination of the observations and returns the relatively stable efficiency scores. The nominal model only considers one situation based on the observation, while the robust model allows some turbulence of the parameters around the moments information, which is a trade-off of a scenario set that may contain the true value happen in future. The proposed model takes account the worst scenario that how far each output can move away from its elliptical center. Thus, the model can predict the changing of the outputs and reflect the truth with a high confidence level. We apply the proposed robust DEA model to handle the impacts of the uncertainty of outputs in the next section.

10.3   Results and Analysis

The comparison from calculations is described as follows. Wu and Wu first solved the nominal DEA model, then perturbed a small amount of each output by 1% around the nominal value for the robust counterpart, finally we varied all outputs with different variation levels, e.g. [±5%; 0; ±3%; ±3%; ±8%], at one time, and obtained the robust efficient scores. Output 5 fluctuates in a larger range than those of Outputs 3 and 4 because the number of patient visits is one of the factors that determine the hospital revenue. Output 2 keeps unchanged as the values of technology index are relatively conservative, and it has the smallest std./mean ratios across all groups in Table 10.3. This setting allows us to capture the correlations between different outputs, which is more realistic in practice. Both models can be solved by interior-point-based approaches. For example, we solved the nominal model by linprog function and the robust counterpart by Sedumi both on the MATLAB platform. The percentile distribution of scores under different models and associated statistical information are listed in Table 10.4.

The nominal CCR model returned 105 efficient DMU, which accounts for 31.91 percent of all hospitals. On the other hand, the robust DEA model can reduce the number of efficient hospitals and make the results more reasonable. As seen in Table 10.4, scenario 1 shows that the efficient DMUs decreased to 27 when Output 1 changed ±1% around mean observation. The perturbations from Outputs 2, 3, and 4 have significant impacts on the efficiency scores, i.e. only 2, 8, and 6 efficient DMUs under their robust counterparts. In scenario 6, the efficient DMUs number decreased to 25 when all outputs are varied within different ranges.

Despite the smaller number of efficient DMUs, the robust DEA model produced most of the scores over 60th decile, which is better than the distribution of the nominal model. For instance, scenario 2 generated the higher efficiency scores with a mean of 0.9043 and a lower standard deviation than the nominal model, which represents 5.19% of improvement in terms of Std/Mean ratio. In general, the robust

Table 10.4 Score distribution under nominal and robust models

Decile	Nominal model	Scenario 1	Scenario 2	Scenario 3	Scenario 4	Scenario 5	Scenario 6
90th	38	171	228	212	221	158	139
80th	52	38	27	28	29	35	49
70th	51	43	37	36	35	44	50
60th	48	31	19	22	20	28	33
50th	15	8	9	10	7	6	14
40th	12	7	3	7	4	8	11
30th	6	3	2	3	6	4	4
20th	2	1	2	1	1	1	3
Efficient	105	27	2	8	6	44	25
Inefficient	224	302	217	319	323	284	303
Mean	0.825	0.881	0.904	0.887	0.899	0.881	0.842
Std dev	0.176	0.158	0.146	0.167	0.152	0.167	0.176
Skewness	−0.842	−1.354	−1.762	−1.846	−1.801	−1.664	−1.170
Kurtosis	3.073	4.294	5.941	6.558	5.851	6.090	3.867

Note: Output varied in percentage: Scenarios 1–5 perturbed $\pm 1\%$ around observations for Outputs 1–5, respectively, while Scenario 6 varied outputs individually ($\pm 5\%$, $\pm 3\%$, $\pm 3\%$, $\pm 8\%$)

model can improve average efficiency scores consistently without deteriorating standard deviation. That is, the adjusted ranking system remains relatively stable when facing uncertain outputs. Finally, the robust efficiency scores generally are more left-skewed and have larger kurtosis values, these are because the robust model makes the scores more concentrated toward the top, and produced long-fat tails with outliers represented by underperformance hospitals. Overall, the score distributions showed that the robust model could generate asymmetric distributions that are more realistic for evaluating a larger number of hospitals.

Wu and Wu displayed the statistical results under different scenarios in Table 10.5, which exposes efficient hospital number and average group performance across the hospital profit levels. The "Std" column denotes the standard deviation of the efficient scores in a specific group, which can be seen as one indicator for ranking the stability of the performance. The Std/Mean ratio, or risk to mean ratio in the context, represents relatively changing given one unit score, which allows us to compare the performance across different groups in terms of risk management perspective. The efficient nonprofit hospitals from group 1 reduced most significantly with respect to the changing of Output 2, while the same trends for the efficient DMUs in group 3 occurred in the perturbation of patient visits. The middle group remained relatively large number of efficient hospitals since they consider the balance of profit and nonprofit performance metrics.

The standard deviations of group 2 are generally great but its mean values are smaller than those from group 1 and 3, which leads to relatively high evaluation risk. It is clear to see associated std. to mean ratios are high in general. However, group 2 also has the best performance regarding small perturbation of Output 2. The robust

Table 10.5 Score statistics across groups

	Group 1	132	Group 2	166	Group 3	31
	Efficient	Std/mean	Efficient	Std/mean	Efficient	Std/mean
Nominal model	47	0.18	47	0.24	11	0.22
Scenario 1	13	0.16	11	0.20	3	0.15
Scenario 2	0	0.13	2	0.19	0	0.13
Scenario 3	4	0.14	4	0.22	0	0.16
Scenario 4	3	0.14	3	0.20	0	0.13
Scenario 5	18	0.15	19	0.22	7	0.17
Scenario 6	9	0.17	11	0.24	5	0.18

model improves the scores of groups 1 and 3 for both mean values and standard deviations. As can be seen, the std. to mean ratio decreased 0.05 in scenario 2 for group 1 and 0.09 in scenario 4 for group 3, respectively. The average decrease by using robust approach is around 7% for profit-driven hospital set. This improvement can be interpreted by that the robust model applies the worst boundaries to eliminate the efficient nominal DMUs and protect against the potential evaluation risk. Since the hospitals in different groups focus on their own performance metrics, the hospital efficiency may be impacted by the uncertainty of specific outputs and our analysis shows that the proposed method reduces these risk impact efficiently.

10.4   Conclusion

Wu and Wu pointed out the evaluation risk of hospital efficiency derived from the CCR model. To reduce this risk, a robust DEA model based on the second-order cone programming is proposed. We show that our approach produced an overall better performance in terms of average score and the risk to mean ratio across hospitals with different profit levels. The current model can be developed as follows. First, other types of uncertainty sets may be used to enrich the robust DEA counterparts. Secondly, with more inputs and outputs added into the evaluation system, exploring the representative correlations and simplifying the input and output structure is a potential topic.

A possible extension of current work is to consider hospital governance. The input and output indicators used in the models mainly measured the passive social responsibility that only requires hospitals to fulfill its market objectives for the stakeholders. Active social responsibility, on the other hand, needs hospitals to do something beneficial out of beneficence duties. One may design suitable indicators, e.g. environmental protection index, to represent active social responsibility and incorporate them into current framework in order to achieve a more well-rounded interpretation.

Hospitals face more dynamic situations with higher uncertainties in the big data era. Data integration and reprocessing are key requirements to evaluate the efficiency of the hospitals, the main body of the modern healthcare system. Existing approaches for hospital assessment either use a single indicator such as the specialization index in Farley and Hogan [6] or apply systematic model without considering the risk derived from input/output perturbation [7]. In contrast, the proposed robust model provides an important alternative to overcome these difficulties by using prior information derived from big data and generate more stable decisions.

References

1. Nayar, P., & Ozcan, Y. A. (2008). Data envelopment analysis comparison of hospital efficiency and quality. *Journal of Medical Systems, 32,* 193–199.
2. SeDuMi. (2003). http://sedumi.ie.lehigh.edu/ (Online).
3. Clement, J. P., Valdmanis, V. G., Bazzoli, G. J., Zhao, M., & Chukmaitov, A. (2008). Is more better? An analysis of hospital outcomes and efficiency with aDEA model of output congestion. *Health Care Management Science, 11,* 67–77.
4. Ozcan, Y. A. (1992). Sensitivity analysis of hospital efficiency under alternative output/input and peer groups: A review. *Knowledge and Policy, 5,* 1–29.
5. Kaplan, S., & Garrick, B. J. (1981). On the quantitative definition of risk. *Risk Analysis, 1*(1), 11–27.
6. Farley, D. E., & Hogan, C. (1990). Case-mix specialisation in the market for hospital service. *Health Services Research, 25,* 757–783.
7. Jacobs, R. (2001). Alternative methods to examine hospital efficiency: Data envelopment analysis and stochastic Frontier analysis. *Health Care Management Science, 4*(20), 103–115.

Chapter 11
Recapitulation

Abstract This chapter reviews the coverage of the book, sorting out the models presented and the potential they have relative to pandemic response planning. We began the book discussing the initial view of the impact of COVID-19. It has been much less deadly than the black plague but has contagion properties reminiscent of that dreaded disease. It has created dramatic problems for government health systems and has severely cramped economic performance. As Chap. 1 noted, what is needed are analytic tools to aid in dealing with the pandemic impact on our economies. These analytic tools are not panaceas and certainly won't cure the problems we face. But they offer tools that might be useful in aiding governments, firms, and individuals to cope with the problems created by pandemics.

11.1 Problem Background

Health and economic development requires the ability to control the spread of epidemic diseases. The current global supply chain network has resulted in highly complex and interconnected chains of supply for practically every product we use. Certainly, supply chain risk management requires alternate sources throughout the production chain. Chinese sources were the first to be shut down, but simply finding alternative sources proved inadequate as a solution. With the international spread of COVID-19, demand collapsed in great part, with many production facilities shut down. Now the emphasis might shift to applying more automation and technology to avoid the risk of human labor. This in turn has massive ramifications with respect to how humans can find means to support themselves.

Regardless of the means of production, firms will need to improve their ability to monitor events through improved information systems. All organizations, governmental or private, must be prepared for the unexpected through increased slack. This is a different philosophy than has been used to optimize supply chain systems (lean is the inverse of slack). All organizations will need to be prepared to react to new information as it becomes available, identifying links in supply chain networks between these new situations, and identify the relationship to previous experience

D. D. Wu, D. L. Olson, *Pandemic Risk Management in Operations and Finance*,
Computational Risk Management, https://doi.org/10.1007/978-3-030-52197-4_11

Table 11.1 Models covered

Model	Category	Chapter	Pandemic example
System dynamics	Simulation	3	Macromodel of pandemic
Sentiment analysis	Data acquisition	4	Social media problem identification
Network analysis	Text data acquisition	6	Detection of disease spread, mitigation success
Financial modeling	Network analysis	7	Contagion network modeling
Information technology	Cloud/block chain	8	Financial policy analysis
Technology acceptance	TAM	9	Health professional adoption of technology
Efficiency modeling	DEA	10	Identification of hospital system weaknesses

in order to evaluate immediate reactions. Table 11.1 displays the types of models covered.

Chapter 3 presented a system dynamics model of financial contagion. Pandemic contagion has similar characteristics that could be modeled with system dynamics. Pandemics by their nature have little historical data upon which to build simulation models. But system dynamics is especially useful in allowing subjective (opinions) of the relationship of virus spread and health treatment systems. We remember the Club of Rome studies [1] that were the initial applications of system dynamics modeling, where economics, pollution, and population explosion were all modeled. System dynamics models cannot prove anything, but they provide a structured way to communicate what particular individuals or groups think, and means to change assumptions as desired.

Sentiment analysis applies data mining to text, seeking to identify opinions. This has proven useful in many areas, to include quality control, customer satisfaction, and financial investment opportunity potential. Chapter 4 shows how this can be applied to analyze Web content or other documents related to pandemic operations. Web crawlers can be used to apply technology to scrape text from social media sources. A support vector machine was presented as a data-mining algorithm useful for complex data typical of pandemics.

Chapter 6 applied Citespace text analysis software to data downloaded from the Web related to past epidemics. Research topics focused on health care, disease, influenza, and infection. The impacts of prior pandemics were all different, in that they tended to have higher mortality rates, but not nearly the contagion found in COVID-19. Network clustering for SARS, MERS, and Ebola demonstrate the ability to quickly gather data on new pandemics, both related to its spread and the effectiveness of mitigation policies.

Chapter 7 applied risk contagion networks to model financial risk. The same could be applied to pandemic risk contagion. The value in identifying key nodes in pandemic contagion is obvious, aiding control of contagion spread. The financial network analysis in Chap. 7 demonstrates some network architecture characteristics related to risk management.

Chapter 8 discussed the financial aspects of the COVID-19 pandemic. The economic recovery of supply chains needs to consider how best to salvage the economy during pandemic spread, as well as to support economic recovery once the health aspects of a pandemic are brought under control. Digital technology is also important. The cloud provides a useful platform for disseminating financial support, applying block-chain technology for security.

Chapters 9 and 10 dealt with modeling healthcare systems. Chapter 9 discussed smart healthcare services. Pandemic planning would benefit from accessing some of the many technology systems available to aid in operations and planning. A technical acceptance model is adopted as a means to consider factors important in the adoption of technology. An example where surveys of doctors provided views of attitudes and perceptions of usefulness of healthcare technology. The ability to communicate across health systems provides a means to effectively coordinate health system response to areas where pandemics deliver the greatest threat.

Chapter 10 applied a DEA model to evaluate hospital efficiency. It was suggested that such modeling could be applied to assess hospital governance. Input and output indicators used in the models mainly measured the passive social responsibility that only requires hospitals to fulfill its market objectives for the stakeholders. Active social responsibility, on the other hand, needs hospitals to do something beneficial out of beneficence duties. Suitable indicators such as environmental protection indices to represent active social responsibility can be incorporated to achieve a more well-rounded interpretation.

11.2 Conclusion

Pandemics create strain on economies, due to the need to provide medical resources as well as the need to control the population to halt disease spread. COVID-19 is expected to have a major impact in setting back global economic development. Obviously, the longer lockdowns are imposed, the greater the economic impact. If some areas of the global economy begin to recover, there might be less reticence to wait before opening up economies on the part of other regions or countries. The choice is complete safety and starvation, or coping with what nature throws at us and move on. It will be interesting to see the relative success of the two extremes on this dichotomy with respect to response to one of nature's challenges.

Reference

1. Meadows, D., Meadows, D., Randers, J., & Behrens, W. W., III. (1972). *The limits to growth*. Club of Rome: Potomac Associates.

The manufacturer's authorised representative in the EU is Springer
Nature Customer Service Centre GmbH, Europaplatz 3, 69115 Heidelberg,
Germany. If you have any concerns regarding our products, please
contact ProductSafety@springernature.com

Printed and bound by CPI Group (UK) Ltd, Croydon, CR0 4YY
29/04/2026
02099455-0017